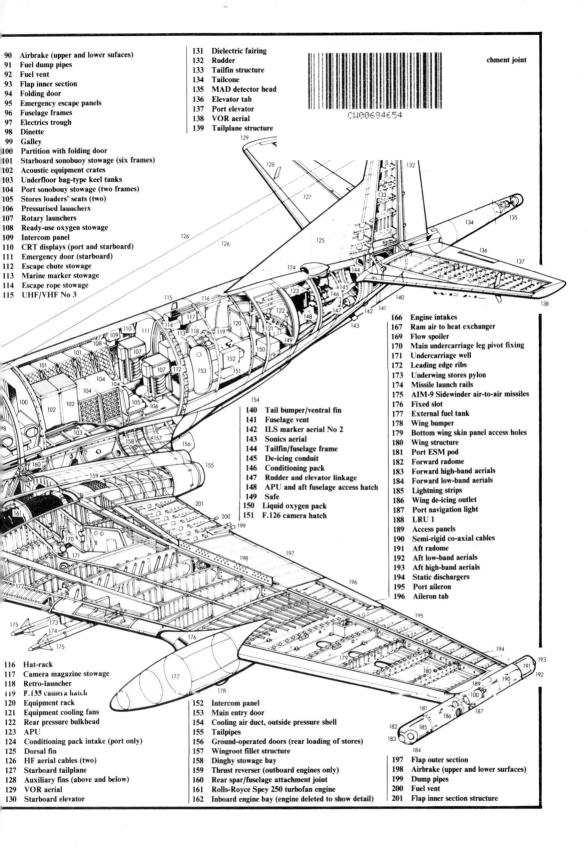

90 Airbrake (upper and lower sufaces)
91 Fuel dump pipes
92 Fuel vent
93 Flap inner section
94 Folding door
95 Emergency escape panels
96 Fuselage frames
97 Electrics trough
98 Dinette
99 Galley
100 Partition with folding door
101 Starboard sonobuoy stowage (six frames)
102 Acoustic equipment crates
103 Underfloor bag-type keel tanks
104 Port sonobouy stowage (two frames)
105 Stores loaders' seats (two)
106 Pressurised launchers
107 Rotary launchers
108 Ready-use oxygen stowage
109 Intercom panel
110 CRT displays (port and starboard)
111 Emergency door (starboard)
112 Escape chute stowage
113 Marine marker stowage
114 Escape rope stowage
115 UHF/VHF No 3

131 Dielectric fairing
132 Rudder
133 Tailfin structure
134 Tailcone
135 MAD detector head
136 Elevator tab
137 Port elevator
138 VOR aerial
139 Tailplane structure

chment joint

CW00684654

166 Engine intakes
167 Ram air to heat exchanger
169 Flow spoiler
170 Main undercarriage leg pivot fixing
171 Undercarriage well
172 Leading edge ribs
173 Underwing stores pylon
174 Missile launch rails
175 AIM-9 Sidewinder air-to-air missiles
176 Fixed slot
177 External fuel tank
178 Wing bumper
179 Bottom wing skin panel access holes
180 Wing structure
181 Port ESM pod
182 Forward radome
183 Forward high-band aerials
184 Forward low-band aerials
185 Lightning strips
186 Wing de-icing outlet
187 Port navigation light
188 LRU 1
189 Access panels
190 Semi-rigid co-axial cables
191 Aft radome
192 Aft low-band aerials
193 Aft high-band aerials
194 Static dischargers
195 Port aileron
196 Aileron tab

140 Tail bumper/ventral fin
141 Fuselage vent
142 ILS marker aerial No 2
143 Sonics aerial
144 Tailfin/fuselage frame
145 De-icing conduit
146 Conditioning pack
147 Rudder and elevator linkage
148 APU and aft fuselage access hatch
149 Safe
150 Liquid oxygen pack
151 F.126 camera hatch

116 Hat-rack
117 Camera magazine stowage
118 Retro-launcher
119 F.135 camera hatch
120 Equipment rack
121 Equipment cooling fans
122 Rear pressure bulkhead
123 APU
124 Conditioning pack intake (port only)
125 Dorsal fin
126 HF aerial cables (two)
127 Starboard tailplane
128 Auxiliary fins (above and below)
129 VOR aerial
130 Starboard elevator

152 Intercom panel
153 Main entry door
154 Cooling air duct, outside pressure shell
155 Tailpipes
156 Ground-operated doors (rear loading of stores)
157 Wingroot fillet structure
158 Dinghy stowage bay
159 Thrust reverser (outboard engines only)
160 Rear spar/fuselage attachment joint
161 Rolls-Royce Spey 250 turbofan engine
162 Inboard engine bay (engine deleted to show detail)

197 Flap outer section
198 Airbrake (upper and lower surfaces)
199 Dump pipes
200 Fuel vent
201 Flap inner section structure

BAe
NIMROD

A familiar but superb photograph of No 206 Squadron's
Nimrod MR2 XV228 over an oil rig in the North Sea.
Sgt Jerry Chance, RAF Public Relations Staff

XZ286 in flight in July 1980. *BAe*

Modern Combat Aircraft 24

BAe
NIMROD

John Chartres

LONDON

IAN ALLAN LTD

First published 1986

ISBN 0 7110 1575 9

Published by Ian Allan Ltd,
Shepperton, Surrey; and printed by
Ian Allan Printing Ltd at their
works at Coombelands in
Runnymede, England

Acknowledgements
In writing about an aircraft of
such complexity as Nimrod,
together with its systems, I have
been more than ever grateful for
the help of many generous and
patient experts within both
industry and the Royal Air
Force.

I would particularly like to
thank Mr R.G. ('Dick')
Proudlove, Nimrod Project
Manager of British Aerospace
Woodford, Mr W.G. Heath,
Structures Manager there, and
Mr Harry Holmes of the
Publicity Department.

Again my thanks go to Gp
Capt T.C. Flanagan MSc, BA
(Hons), RAF(Retd) of the Air
Historical Branch (RAF) and
his staff. At RAF Kinloss I
received a warm welcome and
much help from Gp Capt David
Emmerson AFC, RAF, the
Station Commander, Flt Lt
David Steer, Sgts John Perks
and Paul Warrener of No 201
Squadron, and many others. Flt
Lt E.L. Banfield AFC, RAF of
No 236 Operational Conversion
Unit, and Flt Lt Alec Ayliffe of
No 42 Squadron provided me
with much information and the
loan of precious documents
from St Mawgan.

Mr A.R. Fenn, Public
Relations Officer of RAF Strike
Command, opened many doors
and secured many privileges for
me.

The research on this book was
commenced by Mr Martin
Horseman, formerly of Ian
Allan Ltd, and his impeccable
note-taking and filing
procedures made the potentially
tricky task of a 'takeover' very
easy indeed.

To collectors of Ian Allan
aviation books I may owe an
apology in that there is some
repetition from my *Shackleton*
volume, particularly in passages
relating to the background of
the Nimrod design. This has
been inevitable as I certainly do
not flatter myself that many
outside an immediate circle of
family and friends buy *all* my
books!

John Chartres
Hale, Cheshire

Contents

Introduction

'We Search and Strike'

A one-time unofficial motto of Royal Air Force Coastal Command.

'And Cush begat Nimrod: he began to be a mighty one in the earth. He was a mighty hunter before the Lord.'

Genesis Chapter 10, Verses 8 and 9.

'The undertaking of surveillance operations to maintain a flow of information about the movements of potentially hostile surface vessels and submarines over vast ocean areas.'

Definition of the role of No 18 (Maritime) Group of Strike Command, the successor to Coastal Command RAF after the 1968 reorganisation.

This is a book about an aeroplane which met the requirements outlined above and which was named appropriately. Except that the Nimrod not only became a mighty hunter, but also a mighty life-saver.

Regrettably in the mid-1980s the proud name of 'Nimrod' became primarily associated in the public mind with a very expensive and lengthy 'technical hitch' in the form of the delay in perfecting the radar installation for the Mk 3 Airborne Early Warning aircraft. For some years before the facts about this problem received wide and often adverse publicity, a number of senior RAF officers had been advocating the adoption of a completely different name for this particular Nimrod variant. Their case was validated when an otherwise well informed, though critical, *Panorama* television programme, supported by a *Listener* article, simply referred to the 'Nimrod' project and made no reference to the Maritime Reconnaissance Mk 1s and 2s which had by then served faithfully and efficiently for 15 years and which had made a significant contribution to the winning of the nation's last war in the Falklands. That whole complex subject of Nimrod AEW3 is dealt with in a later chapter.

Although Nimrods and their predecessors are and have been labelled maritime *reconnaissance* (earlier 'general' reconnaissance) aircraft and No 18 Group's role definition above lays stress on surveillance, it

Below:
Nimrod XV227 at Kinloss. *RAF*

Right:
A typical fly-past by a Nimrod on Offshore Tapestry duties.
MoD

Below:
Nimrod XV235 in flight.
British Aerospace

Bottom:
Nimrod AEW3 XZ286 at Farnborough in 1982.
Dr Alan Curry

might have been more honest for the RAF to have used, and still use, the description the Royal Navy uses for many of its submarines: the Navy unabashedly calls these vessels 'hunter-killers'.

Mighty hunters the Nimrods certainly are; mighty life-savers and life-preservers they have also proved to be; but in addition they are undoubtedly highly effective potential killers of enemy submarines and, perhaps to a lesser extent, of enemy surface ships. Whatever the terminology, the evolution of Nimrod both in its maritime reconnaissance and early warning roles can be taken back to the earliest forms of flying machines. Armies and navies first took an interest in balloons and kites to enable their generals and admirals to look over hills and horizons: the carrying and launching of weapons was a later aeronautical development.

In this nation, and indeed in many others, the responsibility for the provision of maritime aircraft has tended to alternate between being a naval and an 'independent air force' one. Sometimes there has been some wasteful overlapping, sometimes even more wasteful inter-service rivalries and jealousies, but more often than not provision has been with the benison of that noted British ability to compromise. The beginnings of the evolution of the airborne submarine hunter-killer could be taken from what some would regard as a halcyon period of British service history when what went on in the air was fairly neatly divided between a Royal Naval Air Service and a Royal Flying Corps.

The 'popular' history of aviation in World War 1 is inevitably dominated by accounts of the aeroplanes, especially the fighters, which operated over the Western Front, so that every schoolboy in the 1920s and 1930s knew a lot about Sopwith Pups, Camels, SE5s, Fokker Triplanes and DVIIs, but not all that much about the Curtis H-12, the Porte Baby and the Felixstowe Fury.

These 'big boats', operating from East Coast bases with Felixstowe as a main headquarters, in fact played a fundamental part in the conduct of that war, and as in so many other spheres, lessons learned were often ignored in high places before another conflict was almost upon us. The flying boats' success owed much to a remarkable Naval officer and designer, Commander Porte, who among other things produced two aircraft capable of carrying single-seater fighters on their upper wings, many years before the much-hailed Mayo Composite of the late 1930s. The story of the big boats of the RNAS – including the fact that in the single year of 1917 40 of them were in action over the North Sea, sighting 68 U-boats and bombing 44 of them – is well told in a recently re-issued book called *The Spider Web* by Sqn Ldr T.D. Hallam (Arms & Armour Press). As in World War 2, and indeed in the Falklands War, the full success of these anti-submarine aircraft should not be measured by actual 'kills' alone, but by the deterrent effect of their sheer presence.

After the creation of the Royal Air Force on 1 April 1918 and the peace which broke out on 11 November the same year, the roles of the RNAS boats were taken over by squadrons of the new Service which constituted the 'Coastal Area' Command. They fairly quickly dubbed themselves the 'Flying Boat Union' with their crews' own tradition of declining to polish their buttons so that they took on a sort of sea-green verdigris hue; they also laid many foundations and established many principles which were to culminate in 'Nimrod', and established traditions which were to be followed by thousands of air and ground crews who served in Coastal Command (formed in 1936 and disbanded in 1969) and up to the present day in No 18 (Maritime) Group of Strike Command, even if the non-polishing of brass buttons one was eventually stymied by the issue of 'stay-bright' ones.

The first significant postwar coastal reconnaissance aircraft to succeed the Felixstowe boats was the Supermarine Southampton. With two wings, two uncowled 502hp Napier Lion engines, two open cockpits in tandem, and three fins and rudders, 69 of them displayed the RAF's ability to establish a 'presence' anywhere in the world between 1925 and 1937. Their memorable flights included a 19,500-mile from Singapore to Nicobar and the Andaman Islands and back in 1929 and a 27,000-mile 'cruise' by four of them in 1927 from Felixstowe to Singapore plus taking in Australia and Hong Kong.

Many of the Southamptons were flown by ex-RNAS squadrons which had added the figures '200' to their original RNAS numbers – thus 201, 203, 204, 205, and 210 handled them as the former 'Navy' 1, 3, 4, 5, and 10 Squadrons. Number 201 Squadron is still flying Mk 2 Nimrods, as is No 206 (originally 'Navy' 6); No 203 Squadron ('Navy' 3) operated Nimrod Mk 1s from Malta until British withdrawal from the Island and its disbandment. No 202 Squadron RAF (formerly 'Navy' 2) at present flies Sea King rescue helicopters.

The Southamptons were followed and supplemented by many other large and staunch biplane boats such as the Blackburn Iris and Perth; the Short Rangoon and Singapore; the Saro London; and then by some moderately successful monoplane boats such as the Saro Lerwick to the almost immortal Sunderland which were supported by the American-designed Catalina, in World War 2. (It is intriguing to note that three of the most successful and long-lived maritime aircraft in this nation's history have been adapted from civil designs the Southampton was a development of a proposed civil flying boat to be called the 'Swan', the Sunderland was a derivative of the Imperial Airways 'C' class Empire Flying Boats, and Nimrod, when all is said and done, is a Comet development. The Short Rangoon – in RAF service from 1931 to 1936 – was a military adaptation of the Calcutta which entered Imperial Airways service in 1928.)

Although aviation history might say that the 'Flying Boat Union' did not contribute all that much to the

Above:
A Curtiss H12 Large America, progenitor of a whole breed of maritime aircraft.

Left:
A Shackleton and a Nimrod MR1, both of No 42 Squadron, St Mawgan, flying past during the Battle of Britain display in September 1971. *Peter R. March*

Above right:
A No 236 OCU Nimrod MR1 and a Shackleton MR2C together at St Mawgan in August 1970. *Peter R. March*

Coastal Command entered World War 2 with 450 aircraft, about half of them in the first-line category. They included some remaining biplane flying boats and the remarkable 'Kipper Patrol' of six Coastal Patrol Flights equipped with Tiger and Hornet Moths. The Sunderland had entered service in three squadrons and landplanes were represented by Ansons, with Lockheed Hudsons about to begin replacing them.

No British aviation historian in his right senses would seek to denigrate the contributions made by the Sunderlands and the Catalinas throughout the war and for many years afterwards. Nearly 750 of the former were built, and flown in action, and the latter type equipped 23 RAF squadrons as well as many others from Allied nations. These two flying boat types became true hunter-killers of enemy submarines, albeit with human eyeballs as their main hunting equipment, but with highly effective offensive armament in the form of bombs, depth charges and machine guns – the last often used in duels between themselves and those similarly equipped on U-boat conning towers. Nevertheless, by the nature of things, the properly shaped hull of a flying boat cannot be as aerodynamically efficient as the fuselage of a 'clean entry' landplane, and as the submarine became more of a threat

black arts of submarine hunting and killing (not possessing such devices as radar, sonar, nor much in the way of offensive weapons beyond Lewis guns and a few thousands pounds' worth of bomb load), it did establish some vital principles. The crews proved the ability of RAF aircraft to traverse not only the whole of the far-flung Empire of the time but of the whole world, to be self-supporting to a very large extent (often carrying their own ground technicians with them), and to make their presence felt in many a minor skirmish.

In the mid-1930s when the concept of the large, heavy landplane requiring something more substantial than grass to take off from and land upon was only just emerging, the flying boat was the ideal aeroplane for such tasks. World War 2 was, however, to see both its zenith as a maritime aircraft and its eventual demise.

to the prosecution of both the European and Far East wars so grew the requirements for longer range, greater endurance, increased weapon payloads and higher transit speeds to target areas. With runways of about 6,000ft available in most parts of the world by the middle of World War 2, the VLR (Very Long Range) landplanes inevitably became the front-liners not only in Coastal Command but in the maritime elements of the Middle and Far East Air Forces and among their equivalents in Allied air forces.

A point often missed by advocates of the flying boat is that it is not quite the sturdy amphibious vehicle that its appearance suggests. Even Sunderlands and their ilk needed reasonably sheltered, smooth water to take off from and alight upon.

Although the strategic importance of defeating the submarine became paramount at an early stage of World War 2 there was no time nor manufacturing capacity to spare to design and produce a 'custom-built' landplane for the purpose. Instead a series of bomber conversions and adaptations had to suffice in the form of Fortresses, Liberators, Halifaxes and, naturally, Lancasters.

With the end of hostilities against Germany and Japan in 1945 the RAF's requirement for effective long range maritime aircraft was scarcely diminished at all. Other potential enemies remained throughout the world and the formation of NATO was in the offing, with special responsibilities for Coastal Command in the North Atlantic itself.

The qualities required of a long range maritime aircraft had in the main been determined by experiences gained in World War 2. They included the fairly obvious ones of range; endurance (not quite the same thing); payload, not only for weapons but for the increasing weight of items of hunting equipment being devised by the scientists and for enough men in the aeroplane to work them all; plus the perhaps not-so-obvious one of sufficient *comfort* to ensure the effici-

ency of large crews spending very long periods in often turbulent air.

Wartime experiences had also dramatically illustrated another vital requirement for maritime aircraft – an 'Air Sea Rescue', later restyled 'Search and Rescue', capability; this was not only on sheer humanitarian grounds but born out of the hard economic fact that in war it is wasteful to allow experienced sailors and airmen to perish unnecessarily.

Most of the requirements demanded from a maritime aircraft at the end of World War 2 were initially met by the Shackleton which was to remain in service for many, many years longer than first envisaged and whose story has been told in an earlier volume by this author.

The histories of Shackleton and Nimrod are inevitably intertwined. The first Shackleton flew in 1949 and entered RAF service two years later. The type has remained operational up to the time of writing this book about its successor. In spite of its longevity and popularity the Shackleton still had its origins in a bomber design and was really yet another compromise solution in the maritime world. As was right and proper in terms of on-going development, the Shackleton had hardly begun its long life before the quest began for something better still to replace it. The search ranged over many existing designs and over shapes still on drawing boards before the decision came down in favour of the Maritime Comet, later to become Nimrod.

World War 2 also identified the requirement for large, not necessarily fast, aircraft with the capability of looking over the horizon not for ships' hulls or periscopes but for enemy flying machines approaching with or without pilots, just above the surface. The name of that particular defence 'game' is 'Airborne Early Warning'. It is a vexed subject in this nation's history, and one in which, as already briefly mentioned, the name of Nimrod has become deeply involved.

9

1 Nimrod Evolution

By the mid-1960s when agreement had been reached that the well-proven Comet 4 airframe was the best basic vehicle for a Shackleton replacement, compromise though it might be, the general rules of the game in the happily still theoretical war between postwar aircraft and submarine had become well established. Submarines had become faster, quieter and larger; a high proportion being nuclear-powered had no need to surface for weeks or months on end. The building of vast numbers of them for the Soviet Navy made them one of the biggest threats of all to the West.

On the side of the aircraft, radar had become more efficient and effective at least against the 'conventionals', and the arts of acoustic warfare in the form of various types of sonar buoys had reached an advanced stage. Other devices under the broad label of electronic support measures had been evolved and were being improved, plus the Magnetic Anomaly Detector (cheerfully abbreviated to 'MAD'), and there was even an intriguing exhaust-sniffer called Autolycus after 'the snapper-up of unconsidered trifles' in Shakespeare's *Winter's Tale*. In addition, homing torpedoes were becoming deadlier, conventional depth charges and 'iron' bombs obsolescent, and defensive armament rated as an unnecessary weight and speed consuming luxury in maritime reconnaissance aircraft. (Some of those trends underwent a rapid reversal during the Falklands war 20 years later.)

Most of the submarine and surface ship hunting equipment was present in the most advanced version of the Shackleton, the Mk 3 Phase 3. However, apart from other considerations, this aircraft had a limited airframe life since the steady increase in all-up weight had called for the addition of jet assistance in the form of two auxiliary Vipers which did much for take-off and low-level performance but little for the longevity of spar life.

The broad requirements for the Shackleton replacement envisaged in the 1960s can perhaps best be assessed by an understanding of what is involved in a typical anti-submarine mission by an MR aircraft. The first phase of the scenario is an interpretation of intelligence supplied by other sources – the likely presence of hostile submarines in a given area for sheer political or strategic reasons, perhaps a chance visual sighting, perhaps in the worst case the first sinking of a surface ship. In most cases a long transit is required from a sophisticated base capable of maintaining a large and sophisticated aircraft. This is followed by a long and painstaking medium-range search at medium altitude (below 10,000ft) employing radar and

electronic support equipment and possibly human eyeballs; then a 'close search' by sonar, probably with the help and co-operation of other agencies such as surface ships and ASW helicopters. The penultimate phase is the launching of weapons, hopefully resulting in a 'kill' or 'kills'; then finally of course, a long transit home to base.

Very high speed is not a prime requirement for such a task; indeed the ability to fly low and slow is possibly a more important one; as is fuel economy to maximise loitering time in the target area. Nevertheless a reasonably fast 'dash' speed for both outward and inward transits is obviously desirable both from a tactical point of view and from the very important one of aircrew comfort and therefore the minimisation of aircrew fatigue.

For the same reasons the ability of a maritime reconnaissance aircraft to ascend rapidly through turbulent weather and remain above it during transit phases is important. This requirement has nothing to do with the 'coddling' of aircrew – there is little point in equipping an aeroplane with the most advanced technology in the world if its crew becomes incapable of making it work properly through tiredness or sickness.

The actual launching of weapons (with homing torpedoes the prime ones to the present day) calls for low level manoeuvrability almost to the point of aerobatics at about 500ft.

These then were the sort of qualities the HM Government procurers had been looking for in a Shackleton replacement. Well into the 1960s the Shackleton still possessed many such qualities but from its earliest days one of its shortcomings had been in the sphere of crew fatigue with typical anti-submarine warfare training sorties over the Atlantic taking 15 or more noisy, bumpy hours with consequent reductions in efficiency at the business end. In addition a whole new generation of computerised hunting equipment was under development. What was needed by the turn of the 1960/70 decade was not only a new 'carrier' for the existing Shackleton internal fit but one which could also be quickly adapted to carry whatever was coming next.

Top right:
An early Comet picture of G-ALVG bearing BOAC nose markings and the Union Flag on the fin. *Central Press*

Right:
'The World's first jet airliner' pictured on 27 July 1949 at Hatfield with a DH108 supersonic experimental aircraft alongside. *PA-Reuter*

Above:
Comet 4s being handed over by de Havilland to BOAC at London Airport on 30 September 1958. *PA-Reuter*

Top right:
An Atlantic or Atlantique – a main contender against Nimrod in the maritime reconnaissance sales war of the 1960s.
Avions Marcel Dassault-Breguet Aviation

Centre right:
A No 11 Squadron Royal Australian Air Force P-3B Orion, another Nimrod competitor. *RAF*

Bottom right:
A Comet 4 of BOAC in flight. *Camera Press*

Those involved at the time in what was then Hawker Siddeley, later to become part of British Aerospace, still say in a sort of chorus: 'We looked at about everything of the right size which was flying and also at some sketches on drawing boards which might be made to fly. Then we came back to the Comet.'

The ingredients which went into what was to become Air Staff Requirement 381 were probably being considered as early as 1958 and a maritime reconnaissance version of the Comet was certainly a gleam in many an eye by 1960. The 1963 'Statement on Defence' including a memorandum on the Air Estimates issued by the Conservative government of the time said: 'studies are in progress of the characteristics required in a Shackleton replacement'.

The preparation of ASR 381 was complicated because the first lines of thought, expressed in AST

(Air Staff Target) 357 envisaged an ever longer span of life for the Mark 3 Shackletons and then a quantum jump into an aircraft/anti-submarine system capable of meeting the very worst foreseeable threat from the Soviet Navy by about 1970. When it became clear that a leap of that magnitude could not be met before the mid-1970s at earliest, particularly in the realms of hunting equipment and weapons, some sort of interim step had to be considered.

Air Staff Requirement 381, out of which Nimrod was born, was issued formally on 4 June 1964. Well before that both the major British consortia of the time, Hawker Siddeley and British Aircraft, plus some overseas contenders, had been taking an intense interest in the Shackleton replacement project against a background of continuing revelations about the growth of the Soviet submarine threat.

In addition to the Maritime Comet concept, design studies considered included the French twin-turboprop Breguet Atlantic, the Lockheed P3 Orion, a BAC '10-11' (a version of the 1-11 airliner with VC-10 wings), a 'shape' called the Avro 776, the Trident airliner, a four-engined version of the 748, and fast and slow versions of the Belfast freighter. Some of the studies envisaged a mixture of turbofan and turboprop propulsion and thought was given to variable geometry as an answer to the high dash speed and low loiter speed requirement.

The intention to order a maritime version of the Comet 4C, initially to replace the 60 Mk 2 Shackletons still in service, was announced in Parliament on 2 February 1965. (A 'maritime profile' assessment sortie had been flown in mid-1964 in a Comet 3 from Hatfield

with Hawker Siddeley design representatives from Manchester on board.) The projected aircraft was given the manufacturers' designation of Hawker Siddeley 801, with military Mk 250 Rolls Royce Spey turbofans of about 11,500lb thrust specified in place of the Comet 4C's 10,500lb Avons as the first material change announced.

Although the decision, announced by Mr Harold Wilson's Labour government, was sharply criticised in Parliament – a former Secretary of State for Air, Mr Hugh Fraser (Conservative, Stafford & Stone), calling it 'nonsensical' – it was generally approved of by knowledgeable aviation writers. The first order was for 38 aircraft for the RAF with two modified standard Comet 4Cs to be available for company development work. A general arrangement drawing was released for publication in August 1966 showing the first distinctive difference in outward shape from the Comet – the 'double-bubble' effect created by an unpressurised weapons bay pannier 'hung' on the familiar fuselage.

Conversion work on the first development prototype (XV148) started at the Hawker Siddeley (former de Havilland) factory near Chester early in 1965 using an unfinished Comet airframe bearing the manufacturer's number 6477. Because this airframe had not been fully assembled when the project began it was amenable to the installation of Spey engines from the outset and became the first 'Nimrod' to fly, all of 40 miles from Chester to Woodford in the hands of John Cunningham on 23 May 1967. It became the handling and performance aerodynamic prototype.

The lower-numbered aircraft, which became the Nimrod second prototype, XV147, was a Comet 4C (Constructor's Number 6467) and was flown from Chester to Woodford on 25 October 1965. The engine installation in this aircraft was (and still is) unique. Avon 525B engines were installed driving constant speed drives and AC generators carried beneath the engines. The initial flight as Nimrod XV147 was from Woodford on 31 July 1967.

The name Nimrod was officially conferred on the Maritime Comet early in 1967 by Lord Shackleton, then Minister of Defence RAF. Mr Gordon Wansbrough-White, a former Coastal Command pilot with a special interest in aircraft and aero-engine names, claims he suggested the name to Lord Shackleton during a Royal Aeronautical Society dinner. However it came about, it seemed a highly appropriate name even if it had been born before by a maritime aeroplane, the Fleet Air Arm's version of the Hawker Fury biplane fighter of the 1930s.

The airframes used for XV147 and XV148 were at the end of the Comet 4C line at Chester and 'the shape' by the late 1960s had of course become almost as familiar and confidence-inspiring as that of the DC3 had once been.

By 1965 when the Nimrod conversion work began 113 Comets of various marks had been built at Hatfield

and Chester including 28 Mk 4Cs. After the disasters of 1953 and 1954, the painstaking detective work which went into discovering the causes, the rectification of the weaknesses and the demonstration of faith by de Havilland in the fundamental rightness of the design, the Comet had become one of the most reliable and best-liked passenger aircraft in the world with more than 1,500,000 hours logged. The RAF had already acquired considerable experience with the type – No 216 Squadron became the world's first military jet transport unit in 1956 with Mk 2s and was later equipped with five 94-seat Service versions of the 4C (officially dubbed C4s). Also, the security-shrouded No 51 Squadron, at the time part of Signals Command, operated Comet R2s, described as electronic reconnaissance aircraft.

The vital statistics of the Comet 4C were:

Span:	114ft 10in
Length:	118ft 0in
Height:	28ft 6in
Wing area:	2,121sq ft
All-up weight:	162,000lb
Cruising speed:	503mph
Cruising altitude:	39,000ft
Max stage with capacity payload:	2,650 miles

In the Comet 4C, therefore, Hawker Siddeley (which had absorbed de Havilland in 1960 and Avro in 1963) had the essential ingredients for a successful maritime reconnaissance aircraft. These included a payload of some 23,000lb to cope with the ASW equipment, weapons and a large crew; a comfortable ride at least during the transit phases for 'back-enders' carrying out tasks requiring a high degree of mental alertness; and both a healthy dash speed and ability to loiter at medium speed because of a modest wing-loading of about 85lb/sq ft, and a sweep-back of some 25° on the leading edge only.

The contentious matter of specific fuel consumption in the turbofan versus turboprop argument was met by the type's ability to economise substantially by reducing to three, and finally two, engines while on-station. The criteria for this procedure is naturally that the fuel weight state should be down to the point where the aeroplane can maintain height or even climb on one if there is a failure of either of the last running pair. This facility was enhanced in the Comet shape by the inboard positioning of all four engines making asymmetrical flying 'light on the boot'.

The theoretical Comet passenger stage range of more than 2,500 miles comfortably compensated for the laden take-off requirement of 6,750ft. In fact in the Nimrod the range figure was more than doubled by extra tankage and the additional urge of the Speys brought the take-off requirement to within the typical RAF 6,000ft runway length.

Top:
Crew members in front of XV148 before its first flight from Chester to Woodford on 23 May 1967. Left to right: Bob Dixon-Stubbs, Jimmy Harrison, John Cunningham, and Messrs Haddock, Johnston, Poole and Palmer. *BAe*

Above:
A Comet 2 of No 216 Squadron RAF Transport Command.
De Havilland

Above:
Nimrod XV148 (without MAD tail boom), flying from Boscombe Down in September 1967. *Peter R. March*

Left:
Mr Gilbert Whitehead, leader of the Hawker Siddeley Nimrod team in the 1960s. *BAe*

larger dorsal fin. The increased dorsal fin area was introduced on XV148 during June 1967 and on to XV147 prior to its second flight. The effect of opening the bomb doors was to reduce further the directional stability.

Nimrods were in fact from the start 6ft shorter from nose to rudder than the 4Cs, a plug being taken out of the fuselage immediately ahead of the wing with a view to this improving the directional stability, and it was also thought that the Electronic Counter Measures aerial fairing on top of the existing fin might help too. In the event the pannier, especially with its doors open, had added enormously to the total keel area and the loss of those 6ft was later regretted.

The other major changes to the profile were the tail boom required to keep the MAD (Magnetic Anomaly Detector) aerial as far away from the metallic mass of the aircraft as possible, and the larger intake areas demanded by the Spey engines. The inboard engines needed 680sq in (a 21% increase) and the outboards 646sq in (a 15% increase) and this led to some redesign of the whole of the wing centre section.

The pilots' windscreen was deepened to improve visibility at low level and eyebrow windows added to assist

Although a superficial glance at photographs of XV148 on roll-out might have given the impression that it was just a Comet 4C with a bulge underneath, there was of course, far more to it all than that, and Nimrod really was a new design rather than a conversion to a new role. Leaving aside the internal changes, the addition of the weapons pannier – which was attached to the fuselage in segments so that load changes would not be transmitted to the pressurised hull – created a foreseen effect on directional stability. The Hawker Siddeley team at Woodford (led by Mr Gilbert Whitehead) had, before XV148's first flight, produced marginal results from wind tunnel tests on this aspect and had prepared a design for a much

NIMROD MR MK2

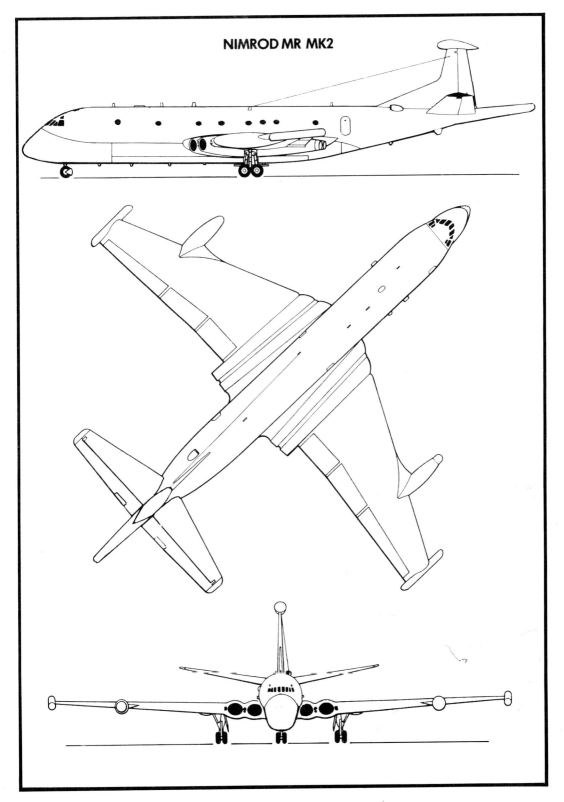

the pilots to look into the tight turns involved in ASW flying. Perhaps with memories of the proven causes of two of the early Comet disasters some very extensive pressure testing was carried out on the eyebrow window installations.

Two wing ribs were strengthened to carry weapon pylons. (At one stage of development, Martel air-to-surface weapons were fitted and tested and others contemplated but in RAF service this feature was not made use of until the Falklands war when it became highly desirable, and quickly possible, to fit Sidewinders for self-defensive purposes.) A searchlight was incorporated into the starboard external wing tank controllable from the cockpit, and the undercarriage strengthened all round from that of the Comet 4C to cope with both the immediate and foreseeable increases in all-up weight.

The essential statistics which emerged for the Mk 1 Nimrod (or Nimrod MR1) were:

Left:
Mr R.G. ('Dick') Proudlove, British Aerospace Nimrod Project Manager at Woodford. *BAe*

Powerplant
Four Rolls-Royce RB 163-20 Spey Mk 250 turbofans: Rated at 12,160lb st (5,515kg) each for take-off; thrust reversers on outboard engines.
Fuel capacity: 8,908 Imp gal plus provision for tanks in weapons bay.

Performance
Maximum 'operational necessity' speed: 575mph (926km/hr)
Transit speed: 547mph (880km/hr)
Economical transit speed: 490mph (787km/hr)
Take-off distance at typical gross weight: 4,800ft (1,463m)
Typical landing distance: 5,300ft (1,615m)
Typical ferry range: 5,755 miles (9,265km)
Endurance: 12 hours
Ceiling: 42,000ft (12,800m)

Weights
Max take-off: 177,500lb (80,510kg)
Overload: 192,000lb (87,090kg)

Dimensions
Span: 114ft 0in (35m)
Length: 126ft 9in (38.63m)
Height: 29ft 8½in (9.01m)
Wing area: 2,121sq ft (197sq m)

Construction
Metal cantilever wings, two-spar with centre-section and two stubs; all-metal cantilever tail; all-metal semi-monocoque fuselage fully pressurised with unpressurised pannier below.

It should perhaps be noted at this stage that all the design features described above envisaged a rapid conversion to a Mk 2 Nimrod once the new internal

Left:
Mr J.G. ('Jimmy') Harrison, Hawker Siddeley Chief Test Pilot in the 1960s. *BAe*

'fits' became available, thus meeting the full requirements of Air Staff Target 357. That in fact started to happen only eight years after the first flight of prototype XV148, although it took a further nine years to up-grade the whole RAF fleet.

Mr R.G. ('Dick') Proudlove, the Nimrod Project Manager at what is now British Aerospace, Woodford, recalls that there were really very few fundamental problems in the design (or re-design) work. The essential element was the shape of the pannier required to turn an airliner into a hunter-killer of submarines. Its dimensions were determined by what the RAF needed to put inside it, and its shape was determined by basic aerodynamic principles. 'Everything else followed logically, and quite quickly, from those two premises', he says.

The new fuselage shape, superimposed on the Comet pressure hull, was in fact created by the requirement first to house the ASV 21 radar scanner, and then looking ahead, the Searchwater scanner plus a Doppler aerial bay and of course, a weapons bay.

The first flight of XV148 was naturally rather more than a straight 40-mile hop from Chester to Woodford. It lasted 1¼ hours with Mr J.G. ('Jimmy') Harrison, Chief Test Pilot for Hawker Siddeley Manchester, beside John Cunningham, and with Messrs S.R. Dixon-Stubbs (navigator), M. Palmer, J. Haddock (flight engineers), J.L. Johnston and R. Poole (flight observers) on board. Thereafter Jimmy Harrison took over the

NIMROD AEW Mk 3

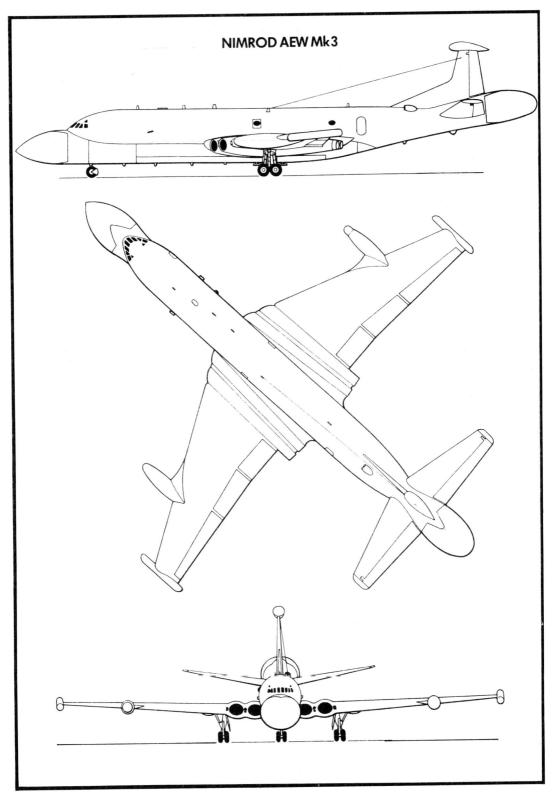

test flying programme and some three months later (by which time XV148 had flown more than 60 hours), he stated publicly that all the evidence indicated that Nimrod was going to be an outstanding aircraft in the hands of Coastal Command crews. In his report, among other things, he said that early trials on engine shut-down and re-light procedures had shown that asymmetric flying, including landing, with the Nimrod was 'completely innocuous'.

The second prototype, XV147, remained in the role of testing NAV/TAC systems from RAE Farnborough.

Hawker Siddeley took on overall responsibility from the start for Nimrod as a weapon system, expanding its own avionics department to cope with the task. Partly because of this policy (which unfortunately was not repeated in the case of the Mk 3 AEW project) the £100 million contract for the first 38 aircraft ordered was at the time the biggest fixed price arrangement with a single company in the British aerospace industry. The production system involved a spread of work over several Hawker Siddeley factories with divisions of the company which had built Comet sub-assemblies making corresponding units for Nimrod. Thus the Chester factory continued building wing centre sections (though the design had been extensively modified to take the Speys) and later took on fuselage sections and outer wings, work on the last being transferred from Portsmouth. Tailplanes and engine intakes were made at Hatfield, assemblies peculiar to HS801 Nimrod at Chadderton, with final assembly and development flying all coming together at Woodford.

The first true 'custom-built' HS801 Nimrod flew in June 1968 bearing the airframe number XV226. It and XV227, XV228 and XV229 became the production development aircraft, all later entering RAF service. Together with XV147 and XV148 they logged 3,600 test and development hours, 1,656 of them in Hawker Siddeley hands from Woodford, the rest of them with the A&AEE at Boscombe Down. In a sense XV227 is still a test aircraft, because although used in squadron service at Kinloss it is permanently fitted with fatigue recording equipment.

The first Nimrod to enter RAF service, with No 236 Operational Conversion Unit, St Mawgan, Cornwall, on 2 October 1969, was XV230. It arrived there just in time to line up behind nine Shackletons in the fly-past ceremony on 27 November marking the disbandment of Coastal Command and the creation of No 18 (Maritime) Group of the new Strike Command. The remaining 33 aircraft in the first order for 38 were numbered XV231–XV263. All but one were delivered on schedule by 31 January 1972, with the last reaching

Left:
The Nimrod assembly line at Woodford. *BAe*

Below left:
Parts had to be brought together! *BAe*

Below:
XV230, the first Nimrod to enter RAF service. *BAe*

Bottom:
XV257 viewed from another Nimrod. *RAF*

the RAF a little late in August of that year because
of an industrial dispute.

A further order for an additional eight aircraft was
placed in January 1972 and delivery of these began
three years later. Only five of them entered service
as Maritime Reconnaissance Mk 1s however. Two of
them, XZ286 and XZ287, were held back for the Mk 3
AEW programme, and XZ284 was built directly to
MR Mk 2 standards. The five which did enter squadron service as MR Mk 1s were XZ280 to XZ283 and
XZ285. In addition three 'specials' were built for elec-

tronic reconnaissance duties with No 51 Squadron –
Nos XW664, XW665 and XW666. They were delivered
by 1973 to replace the Comet R2s used by this squadron for its mysterious duties. Little has been released
for publication about these aircraft or the Squadron's
activities from RAF Wyton in Huntingdonshire but
they are distinguishable by the absence of the long
MAD tailbooms of the MR Nimrods and a curious
shaping of the port wing leading edge pod. It became
known that they were fitted with twin Delco Carousel
IVa navigation systems in 1981 in place of the earlier
Decca Doppler equipment and that their original ASV
21D radars had been replaced with ECKO 290 sets.

Some idea of the complexity and on-going nature of
the Nimrod test and development programme can be
conveyed by taking the work done on the two proto-
types and on the first four production aircraft. In any
assessment of this it has to be borne in mind that
the Nimrod in its Mk 1 form was an interim aircraft
and that conversion to Mk 2 standards was envisaged
from the start. Even the dimensions of the front end
of the pannier or 'blister' were dictated by the size
of the Searchwater radar due to be fitted at Mk 2
stage.

XV148 From first flight (23 May 1967) until January
1969 this aircraft was used for basic airframe and engine development flying from Woodford. Between May
and September 1968 it was used on A&AEE assessment
trials at Boscombe Down, and returned to Woodford
in October that year for further development work.
Then from February 1969 until March 1970 it was
used in preparation for missile trials, also participating
in A&AEE tropical trials between July and October
1969, and between March 1970 and January 1972 the
aircraft was used for Martel, AS12 and SS11 trials
from Woodford and Boscombe Down. In June 1972
XV148 was employed on conversion to Searchwater
development work.

XV147 This airframe has spent its entire life in research and development of the 'innards' of both MR1

23

and MR2 Nimrods. Although it has remained an 'oddball', still powered with Avons, at a very early stage its power generating equipment was up-graded to deliver the voltages and amperages demanded by the equipment put into both the Mk 1s and the Mk 2s.

XV226 This was the first aircraft to be fully equipped to Nimrod Mk 1 standard and was used for the development of engineering systems inside the aircraft, including air conditioning. It was used for both tropical and cold weather trials in 1969 and 1970 and for autopilot development. The aircraft went into RAF service in January 1973 after 281 test flying hours in Hawker Siddeley hands and another 198 from Boscombe Down.

XV227 This initially became an armament development aircraft, some of the work done with it including clearance for the inclusion of long range fuel tanks in the bomb bay. This work was done both from Woodford and Boscombe Down. The aircraft finally

entered RAF service as a Mk 2 at Kinloss but as mentioned above is still a 'test' aircraft under the on-going NOFLMP (Nimrod Operational Flight Load Monitoring Programme.)

XV228 This was initially a Boscombe Down aircraft used for the A&AEE's assessment of the navigational and nav/tac systems. It was also used for weapon system trials in the Bahamas at AUTEC (Atlantic Underwater Test & Evaluation Centre). This aircraft entered RAF service on 6 June 1973, after 852 hours test flying.

XV229 A slightly 'oddball' aircraft, it initially was used for clearance of all the communications systems but later became Boscombe Down's 'hack' development mount for such matters as SARBE personal locator beacon trials and for the communications refit between the Mk 1 and Mk 2. It flew 214 development hours in Hawker Siddeley hands and another 402 at Boscombe before entering RAF service as a Mk 2 in 1969.

Above left and left:
This aircraft, bearing the serial XV814, was originally built as a Comet 4 with Constructor's Number 6407. It was delivered to BOAC in December 1958 as G-ADPF, was later chartered to Air Ceylon and in 1967 was acquired by the Controller Aircraft of the then Ministry of Technology. It has subsequently been used by the Royal Aircraft Establishment, Farnborough along with other non-standard Comets and Nimrods. This aircraft was fitted initially with 'bath tub' or 'canoe' fairings of various lengths and shapes to house experimental electronic equipment. To maintain directional stability with such fairings fitted a standard Nimrod-sized fin was added.

These pictures were taken in 1977, by which time the aeroplane had earned the nickname 'Comrod'. The colourful finish (seen on many RAE aircraft) has been dubbed 'Raspberry Ripple' and was evolved as a protection against mid-air collisions during unusual trial flights, 'whilst retaining some degree of elegance' in the words of an RAE spokesman.

Because numerous radio, radar and avionic trials are conducted in this aircraft it spends a considerable amount of time on the ground being fitted with specialist gear and installations. Nevertheless by August 1985 it had flown some 26,000 hours. *Royal Aircraft Establishment*

Because centralised servicing had become well established in the RAF by the time Nimrod entered service it is impossible to tabulate airframe numbers alongside individual squadrons. The 'users' however, have been and with one exception still are: No 236 Operational Conversion Unit (with a shadow wartime identity of No 38 Squadron) and No 42 Squadron at St Mawgan; Nos 120, 201 and 206 Squadrons at Kinloss; No 203 Squadron (now disbanded) at Malta and Sicily; plus No 51 Squadron at Wyton with its 'specials' designated as R Mk 1s.

No 203 Squadron disbanded in December 1977 after a change in the UK's political relationship with Malta and most of the aircraft it was using returned to Woodford to become the nucleus of the Airborne Early Warning Mk 3 fleet. The first operational user squadron was No 201 at Kinloss which received its aircraft in the summer of 1970 – perhaps an appropriate arrangement since this unit traces its origins to having been 'Naval One', or No 1 Squadron Royal Naval Air Service.

Nimrods For Export
During the 1970s valiant efforts were made by Hawker Siddeley, supported by the British Government, to sell Nimrod overseas. The two honeypot targets were Australia and Canada, with Japan, India, Holland and Brazil offering the chances of smaller but still worthwhile contracts. South Africa and Argentina were also potential markets in those piping days of political peace. Unfortunately the export efforts were all eventually frustrated by a combination of cost-consciousness and defence cut-backs in the nations concerned, a residual prejudice against jet propulsion in a long-endurance maritime aircraft, and by the undoubted excellence of the competing Lockheed P-3C Orion design.

By the beginning of the 1970s decade Australia had already bought 10 Orion P-3Bs to re-equip No 11 Squadron RAAF, but went on considering Nimrod against the much more sophisticated Orion P-3C until 1975 to replace the Neptunes still serving in No 10 Squadron. Apart from Orion and Nimrod Australia also considered an ASW version of the Boeing 707 airliner and, like almost every other Western nation, the Breguet Atlantic. After defence budget cuts in 1974 the field narrowed to a straight choice between Orion and Nimrod, with all sorts of 'offsets' being offered by both manufacturers. The die was finally cast in

Above:
A Canadian Armed Forces CP-140 Aurora, pictured at
Edinburgh during the 1981 Fincastle Trophy competition. *RAF*

Bottom right:
An RAF Nimrod pictured under the tail of the Aurora
demonstrator in Canada in 1979. *Frank Mormillo*

Right:
XV241 in flight. *Rolls Royce*

favour of Orion with eight aircraft ordered at an initial
bill of more than 100 million Australian dollars.

By the late 1960s/early 1970s Canada was seeking
a replacement for its unpressurised, piston-engined
(Wright Cyclone) Canadair Argus which had much
the same merits and demerits as the RAF's Shackleton
– reliable but slow, smelly and noisy, and not up to
accommodating the next generation of ASW equipment. The Canadian LRPA (Long Range Patrol Aircraft) procurers also looked at Nimrod, Orion, the
ASW 707 and at a 'DC 10-10'.

After a series of decision postponements and a nar-
rowing of choice to the Orion and the 707 the decision
was made in favour of the former at the end of 1975
with 18 aircraft ordered. Initially to be called 'Ospreys',
the RCAF Orions eventually entered service in 1980
considerably up-dated and re-named 'Auroras', the
financial deal working out at about 1,000 million
Canadian dollars.

During these and other overseas negotiations a plan
was put forward by some wise men in HM Government
to offer an 'improved Nimrod' for export, perhaps
with an extra engine in the tail to reduce take-off length
requirements. One scheme envisaged the hand-back
of a number of RAF Mk 1s for conversion and overseas sales and their replacement by new-build Mk 2s
to be styled 'Mk 4s'. That intriguing plan had to go
into a bottom drawer.

By 1971 Japan urgently needed a new maritime aircraft to replace its Kawasaki P-2Js plus an airborne
early warning vehicle. Again Nimrod, Orion and the
Maritime 707 were looked at as well as another Lockheed design, the carrier-borne S-3A Viking. Eventually
the Japanese decision came down in favour of seven
Orions, three direct from the Lockheed production
line, another four to be built by Kawasaki from knock-
down kits, plus some Grumman E-2C Hawkeyes for
the AEW task.

A goodwill visit to India was made in 1972 by a

Mk 1 Nimrod from Kinloss flown by a No 42 Squadron
crew from St Mawgan with an eye on that nation's
need to replace its maritime Super Constellations with
at least six new aircraft. The visit did not result in
anything more than goodwill, however, and India
turned eyes eastwards towards the Ilyushin Il-38.

Holland also became an Orion customer in 1978,
buying 13 of the type, while South Africa, the only
overseas buyer of the Shackleton and most certainly
a satisfied customer, would almost certainly have
bought Nimrod as a logical successor, but political
developments dictated otherwise.

The Royal Air Force therefore became the sole customer for Nimrod by the end of the 1970s, but there
was still much work to be done at what became labelled
as the British Aerospace Aircraft Group, Manchester
Division, factory at Woodford. The well pre-planned
conversion of 35 aircraft to MR Mk 2 standards began
in April 1975 and took rather more than nine years
to complete. The conversions took about 11 months
per aircraft with an average of seven at any given
time being out of RAF service and under treatment
at Woodford.

As explained the airframes were ready for the conversion process, nearly all the changes being internal
ones to the tactical and navigation equipment and to
the weapons provision. From the spotters' point of
view, apart from the partly coincidental change from

Left:
Seven Nimrod MR1s of No 236 OCU plus one Shackleton at top of picture, at St Mawgan in August 1970.
Peter R. March

Above:
Mk 2 XV228 at Finningley in 1984. *Dr Alan Curry*

the grey-and-white colour scheme to 'NATO Hemp', the visible external differences between MR1 and MR2 were confined to aerial arrangements, an additional air scoop on the port side just below the dorsal fin and the disappearance of one cabin window. Loral ESM pods on the wing tips of Mk 2s began to appear later as distinguishing features.

The first Mk 2 flight (of XV147) took place in April 1977, and XV236 became the first to enter service on 23 August 1979, its acceptance marked by a ceremony at Woodford in which Air Chief Marshal Sir David Evans, AOC of Strike Command, and Mr Geoffrey Carr, managing director of BAe Manchester Division, participated. The last MR Mk 1 (XV245) was flown into Woodford from St Mawgan on 31 May 1984. Only XZ284, which had been held back from the second contract for eight aircraft (along with two others destined for the AEW Mk 3 programme) could be regarded as a new-build Mk 2 Nimrod. The last-numbered aircraft together with three others was used for extensive trials from Boscombe Down.

The next major tasks for Woodford on the Nimrod MR aircraft were the hasty but highly effective ones dictated by the Falklands War of 1982. The most dramatic of these was the fitting of air-to-air refuelling probes and the associated plumbing, with 16 aircraft dealt with in an average time of 2½ days each. With the RAF the world leader in in-flight refuelling both Hawker Siddeley and British Aerospace had put this facility on offer for Nimrods for several years beforehand and fortunately for the nation everything was ready at Woodford for a quick job using Vulcan probes

and ordinary ground bowser hosing, among other items.

As late as March 1982, only a month before Argentina invaded the Falklands, Mr Winston Churchill MP asked the Secretary of State for Defence in the House of Commons if he would order an in-flight refuelling capability for the Nimrods, and was told: 'It is not clear that the aircraft will need an in-flight refuelling capability; if necessary we shall consider fitting it later in the life of the aircraft'. Fitting the probes might cost about £500,000 each Mr Churchill was told by the Ministry of Defence spokesman Mr Pattie, and would cause disruption in the Mk 2 conversion programme. It very soon became *very* clear that the Nimrod would need that capability.

The fitting involved the loss of the pilots' escape hatch on the roof of the cockpit and added slightly to flight-deck noise. The rest of the crews soon got used to tripping over bowser hose running along the floor of the fuselage but looked forward to the introduction of a Mk 2 version with more sophisticated under-floor plumbing.

The new probes inevitably again affected directional stability in the flying of the aircraft but that problem was quickly solved by the addition of a small ventral fin and 'finlets' on the tailplane. Pilots say that, if anything, the probe-fitted Nimrods are now more stable directionally than they were before the additions.

Other Falklands-inspired changes mainly involved the internal loading of weapons, to be described in detail later, but did include a visible external alteration in the re-fitting of underwing pylons to carry Side-

winders. Rather similar pylons had been fitted to early MR1 development aircraft for Martel or other air-to-surface missiles but had been deleted in RAF service. The strengthened wing ribs incorporated in the original design were still there, however, and made this modification a relatively easy one. (The internal 'fit' of the Nimrod MR Mk 2 compared with that of the Mk 1 will be described in more detail in the next chapter).

The programme to convert 11 Nimrods to the Mk 3 Airborne Early Warning configuration was officially announced by the Ministry of Defence at the end of March 1977, nearly a month after a hybrid aeroplane, XW626, converted from most of a Comet 4C, had been rolled out at Woodford displaying an enormous nose radome but without anything much additional at the tail end. This aircraft was used primarily to provide an in-flight evaluation of a partial Missions System Avionics fit. It also appeared in a number of public demonstrations and photo-calls. Three further development aircraft, XZ286, XZ287 (both of which had been held back from the second MR1 order) and XZ281, entered the Mk 3 programme.

The remaining Nimrods selected for the AEW project were XZ285, XV259, XV263, XZ283, XZ280, XZ282, XV262 and XV261, for conversion in that order. All these aircraft, with the exceptions of XZ286 and XZ287 and the hybrid XW626, began life as Nimrod MR1s, most of them entering service with the later disbanded No 203 Squadron based in Malta. The first production AEW3 (XZ285) was delivered to the Ministry of Defence Procurement Executive in August 1984 and flown regularly from RAF Waddington, selected as the future base for the British AEW contribution to NATO. On 17 November 1980, MR2 Nimrod (XV256) was totally lost in a devastating bird

Above left:
XV237 on approach to Greenham Common in 1983. *Dr Alan Curry*

Above and above right:
Mk 2 XV239 at Yeovilton in 1982, displaying Sidewinders and AAR probe. *Dr Alan Curry*

strike accident at Kinloss. Another (XV257) was
damaged internally in June 1984 following a flare fire
just after take-off from St Mawgan. The only other
accident recorded was a minor one in which the nose
wheel of a Kinloss MR1 failed to lock down and a
landing was made on the foam carpet then available
at RAF Leeming in Yorkshire without serious damage
or any injury. By the end of 1984 the two serious
accidents (the first involving the loss of both pilots)
had reduced the RAF's front-line strength of MR
Nimrods to 33 aeroplanes shared between four operational squadrons and the OCU. Thus the words publicly uttered by Air Marshal Sir John Curtiss, the AOC
of 18 Group in March 1981 – 'We don't have enough
Nimrods' – seemed especially pertinent four years later,
particularly in view of the continuing hang-up on the
radar side of the AEW3 programme which had earlier
taken 11 aircraft away from his command. Sir John,
who had initially spoken out through the columns of
RAF News added: 'I want more Nimrods if we are
going to have to fight any sort of maritime battle,
which seems pretty likely. I mean they (the Russians)
haven't got 300 or 400 submarines just for the hell
of it'.

2 Equipment

To comprehend the complexity and enormity of the equipment placed inside the MR1 and MR2 Nimrods, each single 'fit' costing many millions of pounds at time of purchase, it is best to sub-divide this chapter into the following sections.

1 The aircraft's own navigation equipment, pilot aids and communications, provided to enable it to be in the right place at the right time, and to convey information to the right place.
2 The hunting or detection equipment, enabling it to find its targets either on the surface of the sea or below it – and also to enable it to carry out its most important alternative role, that of saving life.
3 The weapons enabling it to 'kill' if necessary.

Aircraft Routine Navigation, Auto-Pilot and Communications Equipment
Navigation of the aircraft from base to on-station and back is the responsibility of an officer aircrew member, somewhat inadequately referred to as the Routine Navigator. His principal tools are, or have been between Mk 1 and Mk2, the Decca Doppler operating

in conjunction with a Marconi Elliott E3 intertial platform backed by duplicated Sperry GN 7 gyro-compasses and an Air Data Computer. A Ferranti FIN 1012 Interial Navigation System is incorporated in the Nimrod Mk 2 to provide improved system performance and reliability.

A central computer (a Marconi 920B in the Mk 1 and a Marconi 920 ATC in the Mk 2) continually calculates the aircraft's present position which is displayed on the Routine Navigator's tabular display. In addition computed groundspeed and track outputs drive the Routine Dynamic Display. This display optically projects an aircraft present-position symbol on to a chart on the Routine Navigator's plotting table. One of the important fail-safe aspects of this system,

Below:
A 'Routine Navigator' in position at the console of a Nimrod during the course of transit navigation. The officer pictured is Lt John Pfeiffer of the United States Navy on secondment to No 201 Squadron RAF, during a detachment to the ANZUK force in Singapore in 1973. *RAF*

Below:
Nimrod MR1 XV226 seen during an air show flypast and displaying the aircraft's large weapons bay. '226' was the first production Nimrod MR1, which made its maiden flight on 28 June 1968 and then spent over four years on the development programme. It was particularly involved with the trials of engineering systems, and autopilot development and clearance work, before entering RAF service in January 1973.
Peter R. March

very relative to an aircraft like Nimrod carrying out agile manoeuvres at low level, is that in the event of Doppler failure, or during steep turns, ground speed and drift information is still automatically derived from other sources. If inertial platform failure occurs, reversionary true heading is obtained from the twin gyro-magnetic compasses and the variation computer.

If both Doppler and the inertial platform fail, velocity is still obtained from the central air date computer. Heading data can also be up-dated by stellar observation using a synchronous astro-compass and a manually operated sextant.

Other navigation aids available to the Routine Navigator and the pilots include ADF compasses, VOR/ILS, TACAN and LORAN. On the Mk 2 LORAN is being replaced by Omega – a very low frequency global navigation system.

An important feature of all the Nimrod systems is that 'the man remains the master' – machines provide the information but decision-making is still vested in the Brain, Human, Mk 1. For example, the routine dynamic display processes track and groundspeed and the convergence of the earth's meridians to drive an optically projected arrow symbol across a chart which can be on any scale between 1:200,000 and 1:36,000. A tiny joystick control can be used to slew the symbol in the light of new information such as a visual or radar fix, but this adjustment is a matter for decision by the navigator, not by the machine.

Similarly the Tactical Navigator has discretion over what tactical information, from the various sensor systems, is fed into the Central Tactical System. This system performs the navigation and steering calculations and, as necessary, co-ordinates transformations.

The automatic flight control system consists of a three-axis Smiths SEP 6 autopilot and an SFS 6 flight system, both integrated with the total navigation system. The autopilot performance was extended at an early stage to give safe control even when low-flying over the sea. The twin radio altimeters provided can also have their outputs fed into the automatic system.

The communications systems in Nimrod cover every imaginable requirement from the familiar Pye Westminster used to talk direct to lifeboats and trawler skippers or yachtsmen in distress, through fairly standard twin UHF/VHF voice sets, a long-range HF pack (one Marconi AD 470 in the Mk 1, two of them in the Mk 2) up to a low frequency, very long range receiver fitted mainly for the intake of high-grade cypher orders and information. Radio Airborne Teletype (RATT) and Morse inputs and outputs can be used on the UHF/VHF and HF sets and both forms of communications can be received on LF.

Other communications equipment includes the essential personal locator beacon homing set for search and rescue purposes, a Nestor secure voice 'scrambler', and an IFF (Identification Friend or Foe) transponder system which can be used in both civil and military modes.

Hunting & Detection Equipment

The first phase of an anti-submarine or anti-shipping operation – the action on receipt of intelligence from other sources – is catered for by the wide range of communications equipment carried in an MR Nimrod. The AOC of 18 Group located at Northwood can, for example, communicate directly with any of his aircraft, in the air, almost anywhere in the world.

After the second, transit, phase from base to on-station, action involves long range searching by radar and possibly by human eyes followed by the use of the acoustic devices, perhaps topped up by employment of the Magnetic Anomaly Detector (MAD), culminating in the launching of weapons. Other devices under the general heading of electronic support measures may play their part.

From the time of arrival on-station, responsibility for guiding the aircraft to its ultimate attack position passes to another aircrew officer, the Tactical Navigator, who is constantly receiving information via computer from a variety of sensors. The Tactical Navigator, sitting beside the Routine Navigator, controls the Central Tactical System, the heart of the whole Nimrod weapons system. The information from the navigation system and the tactical sensors is processed by the Central Tactical System and displayed to the Tactical Navigator on a 24in diameter display screen. The screen is visible to the Routine Navigator and some of the sensor operators. Additional information is displayed to the Tactical Navigator on a tabular display.

One of the most important advances in the Nimrod Mk 1 to Mk 2 conversion process was the replacement of the ASV 21 radar, which had also equipped the later marks of Shackleton, with Searchwater. Both sets of equipment were and are products of EMI, with origins going back to the H2S sets of World War 2 which altered the whole course of the RAF's bomber offensive for the better.

The ASV 21 could detect large ships at up to 150 nautical miles, vessels under 100 tons at 40nm, surfaced submarines at 75nm and 'snorting' submarines at 20nm. It could be operated at full power up to an altitude of 40,000ft and could be used to detect land masses at the maximum range of its PPI (Plan Position Indicator) display – about 170nm. It could also be

Above right:
As early as 1973 the RAF described the Nimrod's Elliot digital computer and its 24in diameter display screen as the 'heart' of the aeroplane and its systems. This picture shows Flt Lt Graham Warburton of No 201 Squadron in position as Tactical Navigator during a patrol from Singapore in 1973. *RAF*

Right:
This picture, again taken in a No 201 Squadron aircraft during a routine patrol in the Far East in 1973, displays the central operations room of a Mk 1 Nimrod with the joint console manned by the Routine and Tactical Navigators. *RAF*

Below:
The first of the airborne early warning Nimrod AEW3s, XZ286, made its maiden flight on 16 July 1980 and was pictured here two months later during the 1980 Farnborough Air Show. *Martin Horseman*

Above:
Crew Eight of No 206 Squadron brings Nimrod MR2 XV228 round the taxiway at RAF Kinloss after completing a training sortie; seen just ahead of the Nimrod is the plumbing of the aircraft wash system that was installed to provide a shower-type scrub-down of any salt spray deposits built up during low flying maritime operations. Climbing out in the background is a 'circuit-bashing' Shackleton AEW2 of No 8 Squadron from neighbouring RAF Lossiemouth. *Martin Horseman*

Below:
Nimrod MR2 XV234. This view emphasises the added depth of the Nimrod fuselage after addition of the ventral equipment and weapons bays, plus the forward radar housing, to the formerly slim contours of the Comet design. *Peter R. March*

used for cloud collision warning and as a navigation aid.

The official technical description of the transmitter of ASV 21 was: 'X-band with common transmit and receive waveguide system employing pulsed magnetron with 150KW peak output.' That for the receiver read: 'Superhetrodyne with balanced crystal mixers; reflex klystron local oscillator with automatic frequency control or manual tuning facility.'

Much of the performance detail of the Searchwater radar remained classified at the time of writing but it has been generally accepted that it is capable of detecting a submarine periscope (as distinct from a schnorkel mast) at a considerable range and gives an all-round improvement on the figures quoted for the ASV 21. It is also known that Searchwater can produce a visual display of the profile of large ships, thus enabling an instant distinction to be made between a tanker going about its mercantile business and an intruding cruiser or aircraft carrier. The detection of small targets in high sea states is aided by the use of frequency agility plus the addition of a digital computer for signal processing, and plan-corrected presentation and the co-ordination of target and transponder returns are also facilitated by a digital integrating scan converter which presents the operator with a bright, flicker-free picture. Identification Friend or Foe (IFF) systems are integrated for the interrogation of surface vessels and helicopters. Weather and navigation facilities are also built into the system. (Although primarily an air-to-surface radar, Searchwater has also been successfully adapted to the medium range airborne early warning (air-to-air) role in Sea King helicopters of the Royal Navy, two of which were hastily converted during the Falklands War because of the lamentable lack of this form of cover, but which arrived after

the end of hostilities. The Navy now has a full squadron of AEW Sea Kings with modified Searchwater sets housed in external, retractable radomes.)

The basic arts of hunting submarines under water as opposed to catching them while necessarily surfaced, were evolved in World War 1 and World War 2. They are all concerned with *listening* and with man-made extensions of the echo principle of nature. In both world wars surface ships hunting submarines employed listening devices, usually styled hydrophones. In World War 2 the equipment known as ASDIC employed the echo principle with an electrically generated signal replacing and improving upon the sound emanating from a yodeller's mouth – the artificial notes being especially necessary because sound at normal human frequency does not travel through water. (Whales and porpoises do much better with their voices.) Both the hydophone and ASDIC were surface ship weapons but sonar buoys (now usually termed sonobuoys) extended the principles to aircraft shortly after World War 2.

Sonobuoy types can be roughly divided into those which just listen on the hydrophone principle (passive), and those which emit their own signals and then receive the echoes on the ASDIC principle (active). They can then be further sub-divided into directional and non-directional.

Nimrods carry, and have always carried, a great many of all varieties. The evolution of the many types has been a continuous process since the days of the Shackleton and through the Mk 1 and Mk 2 Nimrod variants. In the process many varieties have become smaller, lighter and cheaper, while others have become larger, more complex and more expensive. In general terms sonobuoys used by Nimrods and by any other type of fixed wing anti-submarine aircraft have to be expendable. Once dropped they are seldom, if ever,

recovered, unlike the 'dunking' or 'dipping' buoys used by ASW helicopters which remain attached to the aircraft and thereby are more efficient in certain circumstances.

The usual course of events in the hunting process is for passive sonobuoys to be dropped first, for the fairly obvious reason that they will not disclose to a wily submarine captain that he is in fact being hunted by an aircraft. As the hunt closes in, active and more precisely directional sonobuoys will be dropped. According to design, on impact with the water the main body of the sonobuoy usually floats at surface level, deploying a flotation collar and an antenna for communication with the aircraft. Hydrophones are released from the lower part of the sonobuoy body and sink to a preset depth. Some types of buoy can be 'commanded' by the aircraft.

In very general terms sonobuoys are dropped by Nimrods at heights of from 150ft to 10,000ft. A typical sonobuoy load in a Nimrod can be well over a hundred, including a selection of some or all of the following types:

Jezebel: The well-proven 'A' size, 3ft long, 19lb weight omni-directional passive buoy which has been used in its thousands for many years by the RAF and the Royal Navy.
Miniature Jezebel: 'F' size (Type SSQ 904) which performs the same functions but which is one third of the length and about half the weight of the above.
DIFAR: Type AN/SSQ-53; passive, but directional buoy. DIFAR stands for Digital Frequency Analysis and Recording.
Barra: An Australian-designed directional passive buoy with a high degree of accuracy derived from its

39

Above:
Visiting the US west coast in October 1981, Nimrod MR1 XZ282 was pictured at NAS Point Mugu, California in company with a Lockheed CP-140 Aurora demonstrator. *Frank B. Mormillo*

Top left:
Nimrod R1 XW664 of No 51 Squadron from RAF Wyton seen during a practice approach to nearby RAF Alconbury. *Peter R. Foster*

Top right:
Flight deck view of a Nimrod MR1, XV233, during a 'fish op' conducted by Crew Four of No 42 Squadron from RAF St Mawgan in February 1981. Part of the 'Offshore Tapestry' mission, such operations involved the monitoring of foreign fishing vessels in the various areas of the UK's Exclusive Economic Zone (EEZ). *Martin Horseman*

five 'arms', each of them carrying five miniature hydrophones, all of which deploy at the preset depth.

Ranger: An omni-directional active buoy based on an American design.

CAMBS: The name is an abbreviation of Command Active Multibeam Sonobuoy. Probably the ultimate in sonobuoy development up to the time of writing, it has a high data rate and presents directional information. The hydrophone depth of a CAMBS buoy is adjustable by radio command from a fixed wing aircraft such as Nimrod, thus giving it much of the flexibility of the dunking sonars attached by cable to helicopters.

Size 'A' and 'F' sonobuoys are launched from the rear fuselage of Nimrod by gravity drop from two six-barrel and two single-barrel launchers. The launchers are loaded manually and the aircrew responsible are instructed on the loading configuration by the Tactical Navigator. The instructions are passed through the Central Tactical System to appear on two video displays adjacent to the launchers. Subsequent sonobuoy selection and release is controlled by the Tactical Navigator. The Central Tactical System 'stores' the knowledge of details of the buoy released and its position in the sea.

One other form of buoy is carried – the miniature bathythermal SSQ 36, whose duty it is to transmit

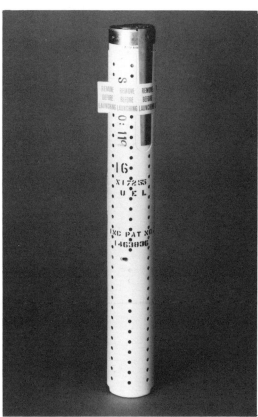

Top left:
A Jezebel sonobuoy.

Left:
A CAMBS sonobuoy.

Above:
Sonobuoy stacking in a Nimrod of No 42 Squadron. This is Master AEOP Cyril Smith in action aboard XV233 in February 1981. *RAF*

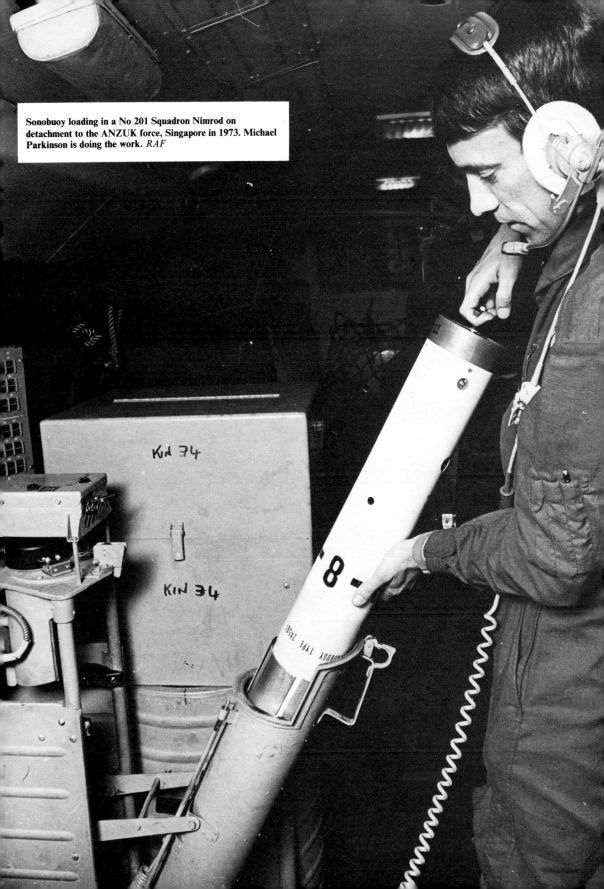

Sonobuoy loading in a No 201 Squadron Nimrod on detachment to the ANZUK force, Singapore in 1973. Michael Parkinson is doing the work. *RAF*

Top left:
Nimrod MR1P XV239 of the Kinloss Wing on finals to RAF Wyton in July 1983. The 'P' in the Nimrod designation denotes the addition of an inflight refuelling probe to the aircraft.
Peter R. Foster

Left.
Still in the Nimrod's original white and grey colour scheme, MR2 XV237 stands on the flight line at RAF Kinloss in September 1981. *Martin Horseman*

Above:
A Nimrod AEW3 fitted with inflight refuelling probe.
British Aerospace

information about water temperatures at varying depths, this sort of intelligence being a vital part of the whole anti-submarine warfare game.

The characteristic tail boom of the MR1 and MR2 Nimrods owes its existence to the Magnetic Anomaly Detector. MAD is a short range location device which detects irregularities in the Earth's magnetic field caused by a magnetic object within that portion of the field being examined. In terms of submarine hunting it provides final, positive evidence that an object, perhaps having first been detected by radar and then sonar, really is a large piece of metal and not a shoal of fish or a whale. In Nimrods, and in other anti-submarine aircraft including helicopters, it nevertheless has its limitations in that the large metallic object below the surface of the sea which it records could be the wreck of some steel or iron vessel of the past, so its information has to be interpreted with circumspection.

The broad subject of electronic warfare remained security-shrouded at the time of writing this book and is likely to stay so for some years to come. Under initial headings of ECM (Electronic Counter Measures), ECCM (Electronic Counter-counter Measures) and ESM (Electronic Surveillance Measures) various devices have been fitted both to Shackletons and Nimrods. The abbreviation ESM meaning Electronic Support Measures was eventually adopted as a blanket label for all such devices. In essence all these devices are concerned with picking up and tracking emissions from an enemy's radar or other forms of electronic equipment, concealing those from friendly sources and generally causing confusion to the opposition. It is ultimately a very complicated guessing game involving such ploys as jamming and counter-jamming, spoofing and counter-spoofing, which absorbs a great deal of mental energy and a great deal of electrical power, not to mention the financial expenditure on the devices

and the payload incurred in carrying them on an aircraft like Nimrod.

One of the distinguishing features of the Mk 1 Nimrod from the Comet 4C was the pod on top of the fin which housed an ESM array. This external feature remained visible after the Mk 2 conversions and initially contained the same sort of equipment. Progressively however, the Mk 2 aircraft appeared with wing-tip pods, the metal centre-bodies housing Loral ESM equipment and the fore-and-aft dielectric end caps carrying high and low band aerials.

The Loral ESM system and the associated wing-tip pods were initially installed on XV241 for development purposes and the initial flight in this configuration was in November 1982 from Woodford. Production installations were introduced on to the last six Mk 1/ Mk 2 conversions at Woodford, commencing in late 1983. The remainder of the fleet has been modified at Woodford and Kinloss.

The tail fin pods have however remained visible on the Mk 2s, partly for aerodynamic reasons, but now only housing 'lumps of something' in the words of RAF technicians, and described as 'dielectric fairings' in official literature.

Pods also appeared in the 1980s on the wing tips of No 51 Squadron's R1s but it has not been disclosed what they contain. The AEW Mk 3s are fitted with pods containing the same equipment as the MR2s.

One of the most important items incorporated into the Nimrod MR2 has been the Marconi-built AQS 901 Acoustic Processing & Display System which in essence absorbs all the information obtained from sonobuoys, processes it in the air, displays it to all concerned on board the aeroplane and also stores it for later study at base.

The AQS 901 system, adopted almost simultaneously by the Royal Australian Air Force for its

Far left:
**The sonobuoy loading and discharge
area of a Mk 1 Nimrod.** *BAe*

Left:
**Paul Rayner (right), Divisional
Manager of the Maritime Aircraft
Systems Division of Marconi Avionics,
and his Technical Manager,
Bob Wilkinson, with the AQS 901
system at the company's Rochester
factory.** *GEC-Marconi*

Below:
Views of the back-end of a Nimrod. *BAe*

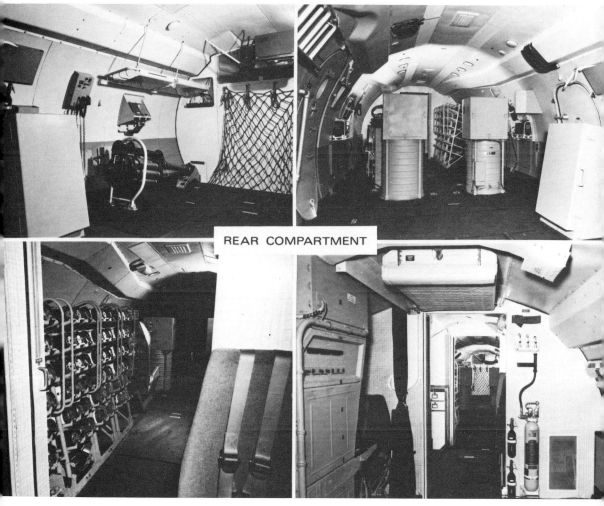

REAR COMPARTMENT

Top:
The Nimrod first prototype, XV148, at the Thurleigh airfield of RAE Bedford in October 1979. *Peter R. Foster*

Above:
With the ground crew conducting exterior checks of the aircraft before opening the engine bay doors and examining the power plants and related equipment, Nimrod MR2 XV228 undergoes an operational turn-round at RAF Kinloss.
Martin Horseman

Left:
Loading search and rescue (Lindholme) gear. *MoD*

Above:
'Bombing up'. *BAe*

Orion P-3Cs, was described at its public unveiling in May 1979 as 'the most advanced production system of its type in the world', which would bring about a quantum jump in the capability of aircraft fitted with it to detect and attack enemy submarines. During that ceremony Mr Paul Rayner, Manager of Marconi Avionics Ltd's Maritime Aircraft Systems Division, explained to guests that a shoal of shrimps could be noisier than a submarine's propellers. The problem was to analyse the received signals from sonobuoys very rapidly and to present to an operator on the aircraft the information he needed to identify and locate the submarine. All this, Mr Rayner claimed, could be done by the AQS 901 system – enabling the crew of a maritime reconnaissance aircraft to 'find the hidden needle in the acoustic haystack'.

The company handout issued at the time said: 'The system contains receivers, digital data processors, controls and displays on which processed information about a submarine is presented to an operator. When in service AQS 901 will be the world's most advanced system of its kind, capable of detecting and locating even the quietest, fastest types of nuclear submarine, operating at great depth.'

The statement went on: 'The importance of airborne detection in anti-submarine defence, lies in the ability to cover large areas of ocean and extensive coastlines covertly and with the maximum of protection against surprise enemy action. The new system represents a major technical advance in that the signals, which are received by the aircraft from sonobuoys dropped in the water, can be processed very rapidly, to give more

49

precise information on submarines than has hitherto been available.'

Those were all wise words in the light of the unexpected shooting war which was to involve MR Nimrods three years later.

One of the important features of the AQS 901 deal, involving as it did, Australia, was that the remarkable Barra sonobuoy, Australian-invented and designed, was linked into both the Nimrod and Orion systems from its outset.

Other vital elements of the Nimrod weapon system are the sensor computers feeding information to the Central Tactical System. For example, on the Mk 2 aircraft, twin 920 ATC computers in the acoustic system, a 920 ATC computer in the ESM system and a Ferranti FM 1600D in the Searchwater radar system all interact with a 920 ATC computer in the Central Tactical System. This input of sensor information together with navigation data, is presented to the Tactical Navigator on his 24in display. The displayed information presents an overall picture of the scenario outside the aircraft in terms of sensor derived intelligence relative to the position of the aircraft, and permits the Tactical Navigator to plan his tactics, leading to weapon release if necessary.

Weapons and Other Stores

Although the original Nimrod bomb-bay pannier was designed to house a mixture of torpedoes, conventional depth charges and mines, the torpedo emerged down the years as the prime anti-submarine, and to some extent anti-surface ship, weapon. Nevertheless a variety of other weapons have been, are or can be carried in the aircraft and launched from it.

These range from the re-introduced 1,000lb 'iron' bombs hastily loaded for the Falklands war (but only dropped on training exercises) to those associated with the Nimrod's publicly admitted 'nuclear potential'. Enough material was published in the 1980s to indicate to any intelligent reader of aviation journals, let alone potential spies, that Nimrods can be equipped with American-made and American-issued nuclear 'depth bombs'. This aspect of the Nimrod's capability of course remains shrouded in security at the time of writing but many invited visitors to the flight decks of Nimrod MR2s have noted the presence of both black and *red* firing buttons on the control yokes.

A typical torpedo load in a Nimrod has been, and still is, a mix of up to nine such weapons. Originally in the Mk 1s and to some extent in the Mk 2s these consisted of the American-designed but British-built Mk 44s and the wholly American Mk 46s, both types homing weapons. The now obsolete Mk 44 was a 'lightweight' torpedo, electrically-propelled, weighing about 233kg, 2.56m long and 324mm in calibre. It contained active acoustic homing devices. The Mk 46 torpedo has also been described as lightweight, but is also a deep-diving, high-speed weapon fitted with an active/

passive acoustic homing system specifically intended for use against submarines. After water entry the Mk 46 can search for, acquire and then attack, its target. If a Mk 46 misses its initial target it is capable of multiple re-attacks. It is 2.67m long and weighs about 258kg. A number of improvements to the Mk 46 torpedo have been going on up to the time of writing with Nimrods as the trial-launching aircraft under 'Neartip' (Near-term Improvement Programme).

Nimrods have also been closely associated with the development of the British Marconi Stingray lightweight anti-submarine torpedo. This weapon, coming up to proven status at the outbreak of the Falklands War, was carried by Mk 1 and Mk 2 Nimrods during the conflict even though it had not been fully proved. Stingray includes an on-board computer to control the homing system, sophisticated target detectors and a special capability to defeat countermeasures. A high performance in both shallow and deep water and general reliability are also claimed.

For many years Nimrod crews trained with the torpedo as the main, and to most intents and purposes, the sole, offensive armament, but the adaptability of the whole aircraft design was proved under the challenges of the Falklands war. A great many other weapons apart from torpedoes were loaded into Nimrods at very short notice when the threat of that war became apparent, more still when it actually broke out.

In the significant period of early 1982 it had been appreciated that the main armament of MR aircraft, consisting of torpedoes designed to kill submarines below the surface, might not be all that effective against either surface vessels nor indeed against surfaced sub-

marines, so the 'iron' bomb came into its own again in the form of 1,000-pounders loaded into the Falklands war Nimrods. Perhaps one of the most dramatic of the many simple improvisations which contributed to success in the Falklands (even if again it was not used 'in anger') was the bomb sight designed and produced in short time at Boscombe Down for the Nimrods.

This device is illustrated. The story is told of a team being despatched from Kinloss to Boscombe Down to collect the sights and the Chief Technician in charge telephoning his immediate boss to say he had taken collection and was on his way back. The telecon is reported to have said: 'Are they analogue or digital?'. Answer: 'They are bits of Perspex with lines scratched on them.' So they were; and what is more they worked. A former Vulcan captain, transferred to Nimrods, tried the sight out on a bombing range near Kinloss and achieved a 25-yd grouping compared with his best 50-yarders using much more sophisticated equipment in his former aeroplane type. A close study of the emergency Nimrod bomb-sight indicates that it had some antecedents in the Barnes Wallis Dam-busters' equipment, but the records remain silent about who designed it and produced it in short time at Boscombe Down. Anyway, it was done, and it would undoubtedly have worked if the necessity had arisen, which happily it did not.

As referred to briefly, provision was made in the earliest Nimrods for under-wing pylon-mounted air-to-surface missiles such as Martels or AS12s. The desirability of some air-to-air protective weaponry became apparent early in the Falklands campaign and with the strengthened wing ribs still available it became a fairly easy matter to instal Sidewinder AIM-9Gs and AIM-9Ls, this work being carried out at Woodford and Kinloss on aircraft destined to go into action in the South Atlantic in 1982.

Among the most important additions to the Nimrod's Falklands weaponry were McDonnell Douglas Harpoon air-to-surface missiles with an over-the-horizon capability. Although not used in anger the loading of two per aircraft provided potential for strikes against surface shipping had the occasion arisen.

Above left:
A Nimrod flight deck scene, photographed in a No 201 Squadron MR 1 while in Singapore on detachment to ANZUK in 1973. Sqn Ldr John Postlethwaite is on the right and Flt Lt Sandy Duthie on the left. *RAF*

Below and below right:
The 'iron bomb' sight produced rapidly at Boscombe Down for the Nimrods going into action during the Falklands war. *RAF*

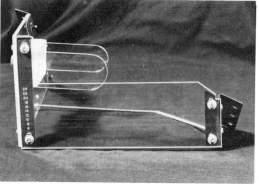

51

The performance of Nimrod-launched Harpoons has subsequently been tested extensively on the United States Navy range in the Bahamas.

A brave attempt was also made during the Falklands War to include 'Paveway' laser-guided bombs in the Nimrod weapon load, but, by a matter of inches, they would not fit into the panniers. Items of miscellaneous stores include a wide range of marine markers in the form of flares and smoke dischargers – some combining both principles – which are of great importance both during anti-submarine and anti-shipping strike procedures and also during search and rescue operations. A feature of the launching equipment provides for flares and other markers to be launched at a 'retro-angle' so that the trajectory corresponds with the forward movement of the aircraft with the net result that they arrive on the water at a point directly below that which the aeroplane is occupying at the moment of flare/marker discharge. This facility is particularly

Top:
An early attempt to give Nimrods an air-to-surface capability: a Martel missile underwing fitting. *Peter R. March*

Above:
Nimrod XV148 with underwing Martels landing at Boscombe Down in March 1971. *Peter R. March*

Right:
Nimrod MR1, XV226, hangared for a routine service at RAF St Mawgan in October 1980. *Martin Horseman*

Far right above:
A Nimrod with weapon loads displayed. The layout consists of Lindholme rescue gear, Mk 46 torpedoes, 1,000lb 'iron' bombs, cluster bombs, Mk 44 torpedoes, Sidewinder missiles, various sonobuoys, and miscellaneous training stores.

Far right below:
1,000lb 'iron' bombs and Mk 46 torpedoes being loaded on to a Nimrod MR2 with refuelling probe at Kinloss during the Falklands war. *RAF*

helpful when an aircraft captain wants to turn back on his own marker either during Search and Rescue or more belligerent operations.

Other stores items include dispensers of 'Chaff' (called 'window' in World War 2) to confuse enemy radar. Cameras too are of course essential reconnaissance aircraft equipment and the normal scale in a Nimrod consists of a mix of hand-held instruments and fitted F126s and F135s made by Aeronautical & General Instrument Ltd. The hull design provides for photography to be carried out through bubble windows at pressurised heights and through opened windows at low level.

Mk 2 Nimrods carry Marconi Avionics ACTs (Airborne Crew Trainers) with which realistic exercises can be set up for the crews during long transits, making inevitably expensive training sorties more cost-effective.

The Lindholme rescue equipment, which replaced airborne lifeboats at a fairly early stage in the postwar development of maritime reconnaissance aircraft, will be described in more detail in a later chapter. Every Nimrod in the air has one set of this equipment aboard and those on specific search and rescue stand-by carry two.

All the equipment described above clearly calls for a substantial amount of electric power to drive it, and so Nimrod is a flying generating station. Power supplies include 200V ac; 115V ac; 28V dc; 24V dc (from batteries); and 26V ac. The main 200V power supply is obtained from four generators, the Military Spey 250 engines being provided with modified gearboxes from the outset. From the MR1 stage onward the generating system was designed to provide additional power as more equipment needing it was evolved. The power take-off arrangements from the main engines are such that adequate capacity is always available even during the shut-down conditions required for fuel economy or in the event of one or more engine failures.

The equipment obviously also calls for a substantial number of people to work it. Nimrod MR1s originally carried 11-man crews and this figure has built up to 13 in the MR2s, including two pilots, a Flight Engineer, a Routine Navigator, a Tactical Navigator, an Air Electronics Officer and a back-end team of seven Air Electronics Operators, usually warrant officers or sergeants and split into 'wets' and 'dries' according to whether they are working the acoustics equipment or other systems such as radar or MAD.

Right:
The Marconi ACT-1 Air Crew Trainer provides cost-effective training facilities for Nimrod crews during transit flights. Mr Peter Hyde, the Marconi Avionics Project Manager, and Joanna Moore, the Project Leader, are seen here with the device which can be fed into the Nimrod MR2s' AQS 901 systems providing exercise situations in which a submarine's attempts to evade detection can be simulated. Sometimes unkindly described as an advanced form of TV game, the ACT-1 is an important feature of all Nimrod training sorties and adds greatly to the efficiency of aircrews. Some, who enjoy their sleep on transit flights, are apt to say, however, that they wish it had not been invented. *Marconi Avionics*

Below:
The Flight Engineer at his console on a Nimrod from No 201 Squadron while on a detachment to the ANZUK force in Singapore in February 1973. *MoD*

3 Maritime Reconnaissance Operations and Training

The location of RAF stations Kinloss and St Mawgan dates back to Shackleton days and before – they have always been ideal jumping-off places for long patrols into the Atlantic and the North Sea, have good weather records and long 'Coastal' traditions. Both are complex bases housing substantial communities of Service men and women and civilians, are important contributors to the local economies of Morayshire and Cornwall and by the nature of the business conducted from them have a distinct operational atmosphere, even in peacetime.

Kinloss not only houses Nos 120, 201 and 206 Squadrons but a number of important lodger units which apart from technical back-up provide for a considerable amount of development and experimental work and for computer storage of the vast stock of information which the Nimrods draw from the sea every day of the year. As well as fairly typical operations and administration wings Kinloss houses one of the largest engineering wings in the RAF. In addition it is the home of the Nimrod Major Servicing Unit, an AEDIT (Aircraft Engineering Development & Investigation Team) and the Maritime Acoustic Analysis Unit.

The operations wing includes a simulator squadron. The engineering wing is broken down into engineering, engineering operations, electrical engineering, mechanical engineering and line squadrons, which together with the NMSU can handle everything up to 3rd-line repairs and servicing, 4th line work going to British Aerospace at Woodford.

The work of MAUU (Maritime Acoustic Analysis Unit) is as its title suggests concerned with the examination and storage of the information obtained on

Below:
A typical 'back-end' crew scene. *RAF*

Above and left:
A Nimrod simulator at St Mawgan. *MoD*

Top right:
Night readiness. Mk 1s in the 'old' colour scheme. *MoD*

Centre right:
The Soviet 'Moskva' class helicopter cruiser *Leningrad* off the Scottish coast. *RAF*

Bottom right:
A Nimrod over a Russian 'Kotlin' class destroyer. *RAF*

every sortie by sonobuoys and other systems about water conditions such as temperatures and salinity levels down to the noises made by oil rigs, those of the conversations of whales and porpoise, and the behaviour patterns of schools of shrimps. Its findings are inevitably heavily classified.

St Mawgan houses No 42 MR Squadron, still semi-officially bearing its torpedo bomber designation dating back to its Vildebeeste and Beaufort days, and No 236 Operational Conversion Unit. The latter organisation resumed this title in 1970, having become designated No 1 Maritime Operational Training Unit in the Shackleton era on merger with the School of Maritime Reconnaissance. The OCU has a shadow wartime operational title of No 38 Squadron.

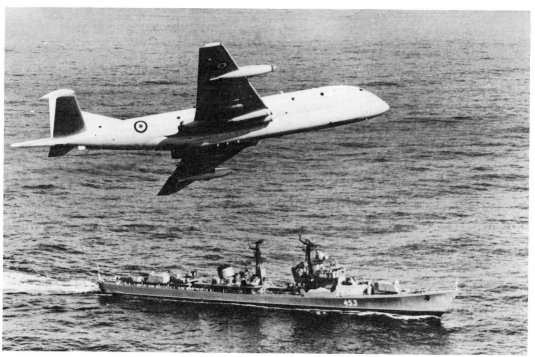

St Mawgan of course has its own engineering wing and simulator facilities and its aircraft normally only go to Kinloss for 3rd line servicing and repairs. Both bases are under command of No 18 Group at Northwood.

The COs of each of the four MR squadrons hold wing commander rank and each squadron is broken down into an 'A' Flight commanded by a squadron

Right:
Crests and badges are normally only worn by centrally serviced Nimrods on special occasions. These markings were on XV246 of No 120 Squadron. *RAF*

Below:
The No 120 Squadron crew which represented the RAF in the 1980 Fincastle Trophy competition. *RAF*

Top right:
Nimrod MR2 XV232 off the South Australian coast during the 1981 Fincastle Trophy competition. *RAAF*

Bottom right:
The winning crew from No 42 Squadron after the 1984 Fincastle Trophy competition. The captain (centre, holding Trophy) was Flt Lt Nick Jones. *RAF*

Above:
Nimrod MR1s at Akrotiri, Cyprus, in 1980. *RAF*

Above right:
A No 203 Squadron aircraft (XV228) over Grand Harbour Valetta in 1977. *Flt Lt A.S. Thomas*

Right:
Mk 2 XV228 at Finningley in 1984. *Dr Alan Curry*

leader comprising between seven and nine air crews; and a 'B' Flight dealing with administration, organisation and security matters. Leaders of the Pilot, Air Electronics, Navigation and Engineering aircrew members are usually squadron leaders. Squadron and flight commanders are frequently Navigators and sometimes Air Electronic Officers.

The operational atmosphere sensed on the bases comes about (even leaving on one side the search and rescue and 'Tapestry' activities described in the next chapter) because the lines between training and live maritime reconnaissance sorties are very much blurred in so-called peacetime. Some security inevitably shrouds this aspect of life in the Nimrod squadrons but the photographs of Soviet vessels at sea frequently released for publication by the Ministry of Defence, especially during major exercises, tell their own story. All this makes for high morale among air and ground crews and a healthy sense of competition exists between Nos 42 (Torpedo Bomber), 120, (which prefers to label itself CXX), 201 and 206 Squadrons, the last two with proud inheritances from Nos 1 and 6 Squadrons Royal Naval Air Service.

This essential element of competition has been further stimulated for many years by the awards of the Aird Whyte and Fincastle trophies. Both trophies were presented by the parents of Sgt Nairn Fincastle Aird Whyte who was killed in action in 1943 while serving as a Coastal Command air-gunner.

The Aird Whyte Trophy is traditionally presented to the Coastal Command, later 18 Group, crew putting

up the best performance in a series of tests in the art of anti-submarine warfare. The squadron whose crew wins this trophy then goes forward the same year to represent the Royal Air Force in the Fincastle competition which is open to the MR elements of the British, Australian, New Zealand and Canadian air forces.

The opportunities for the excitement and challenges of overseas tours and detachments began to decline somewhat for the Nimrod crews with the shrinking of UK commitments in the Middle and Far East that followed soon after the introduction of the type into service. One of the first squadrons, No 203, had to be disbanded after the British political withdrawal from Malta. Nevertheless, as late as November 1971 two crews of No 206 Squadron flew to Tengah for training in tactics and co-operation with the ANZUK (Australia, New Zealand, UK) Force in Singapore and in January 1972 the squadron opened up a Nimrod Maritime Detachment there to replace No 204 Squad-

ron's Far East Detachment of Mk 2 Shackletons at Changi.

As described later, Nimrods are often detached overseas in the 'top cover' search and rescue role for Royal and VIP flights, but the main interest for the operational squadrons now lies in detachments on 'Rum Punch' exercises to an under-sea weapon range off the Bahamas – plus of course continued occasional activities in the South Atlantic. The 'Rum Punch' range, technically 'owned' by the United States, contains the right sort of deep water close to the shore for exercises involving weapon launching against submarines, and a great deal of realism up to James Bond standards can be achieved there in fairly idyllic surroundings.

Visitors to the squadrons sometimes note that the ages of the aircrew they meet and fly with seem to range from the late 'teens to the middle 50s. There are several reasons for this. The make-up of a typical 13-man Nimrod MR crew calls for a great many qualities ranging from youth and enthusiasm to wisdom and experience. Because the aircraft is a relatively comfortable one to work in, with an airliner environment (albeit a rather acrobatic one), medical categories can be fairly wide. The necessity to wear spectacles is no bar, for instance. One Sergeant Air Electronics Operator who had to have a leg amputated remained flying at Kinloss, was later commissioned and then moved over temporarily to AEW Shackletons at Lossiemouth.

The training for Nimrod aircrew at No 236 OCU lasts a standard $5\frac{1}{2}$ months. It covers, in addition to 'conversion to type', such matters as the airways procedure of the transport force, tactical handling and weapons training akin to that of the fast-jet force, and the large subject of MOPS (Maritime Operations). In addition, flight deck and back-end crews have to learn procedures to be used against surface and submerged targets; ship, submarine and aircraft recognition; and the assessment of all the 'opposition's' capabilities.

During the MR1/MR2 Nimrod conversion period a small team from No 236 OCU worked at BAe Wood-

Above:
No 201 Squadron in August 1981.

ford to form the nucleus of a special training unit. When the first MR2s were delivered it became the NCF (Nimrod Conversion Flight) and was located at Kinloss as an out-station of No 236 OCU. In this process the number of converted crew stayed just ahead of the number of converted aircraft. The OCU continued to train students on Mk 1 aircraft while this was going on, but steadily fed its executives and some QFIs (Qualified Flying Instructors) through the Nimrod Conversion Flight to facilitate the eventual training of all newcomers on to the Mk 2.

Since all the early Mk 2 aircraft were delivered to Kinloss the OCU started its conversion courses there and for a time the unit was split between an element completing the final Mk 1 courses at St Mawgan and an advance party at Kinloss.

In the middle of this period the Argentinians invaded the Falkland Islands. A No 236 OCU historian wrote later:

'In view of the situation of the Falkland Islands and the relative proximity to Argentina and its Navy and Air Force, there was an obvious requirement for a Maritime Patrol and Reconnaissance presence. But how could the Nimrod get there and remain long enough to be effective? If it was to be operated in a hostile air environment how could we protect it?

'If it would be required to attack surface contacts it had no suitable weapons: the Shackleton depth charges had long disappeared from the armoury and the AS12 missile had come and gone – thankfully.

'The whole conflict brought immediate activity to the armed services and large areas of industry, not the least to 18 Group's Nimrod Force. New developments came thick and fast and OC 236 OCU was charged with implementing and co-ordinating all the new training required. Just about everything required of the maritime force in the South Atlantic would be "new ground".'

No 236 OCU's historian's remarks above are quoted in full to show what an important part this sometimes under-recognised unit played in the Falklands victory. Throughout the Nimrod force of 18 Group however, intense activity went on in those spring weeks in 1982. Like all the other elements of the British armed forces, the Nimrod air and ground crews and their 'supporters' were at least half-ready for something of the sort happening somewhere in the world, and all the talents of quick reaction, ingenuity, ability to improvise and perhaps most importantly esprit de corps were avilable to help the Government and the nation.

One of the many factors contributing to victory in the Falklands was the RAF's expertise in the art of

Left:
Nimrod MR2s of all four front-line squadrons flew numerous sorties during the large Soviet navy 'blue water' exercise in July 1985, and hundreds of photographs were taken. This view shows an aircraft of No 120 Squadron over a Russian frigate. Reports in a national Sunday and a national daily newspaper that a No 42 Squadron Nimrod had 'disguised' itself as a civilian airliner were of course proved to be totally erroneous and corrected before serious diplomatic damage was done.
Kevin Holt, Daily Mail

Below:
A No 42 squadron MR1 in hemp camouflage at Gibraltar during the 1981 'Springtrain' exercise. A USN P-3 Orion is in the background. *RAF*

air-to-air, or in-flight, refuelling. Sir Alan Cobham, the World War 1 pilot, world record-breaker and air circus owner, had tried to sell the idea for nearly 30 years, nearly succeeded when it was thought that the conventional bombing of Japan would be necessary, and finally succeeded when it became necessary for the RAF to keep its V-bombers aloft for long periods and later to carry out rapid reinforcement exercises with Lightnings to the Far East during the UK withdrawal period. At about the same time the Royal Air Force won the Transatlantic Air Race with its Harriers using the Alan Cobham system and went on perfecting it, but mainly for the refuelling of fighters and V-Bombers rather than large transport or maritime reconnaissance aircraft. The RAF technique of AAR had however reached a fairly advanced stage by 1982 and was rapidly accelerated during the build-up to the Falklands conflict.

In the Nimrod world there were two immediate requirements – firstly to get some aircraft to Ascension Island in order at least to give some MR cover to the ships and aircraft operating from that base during the build-up, and then to up-gun the aeroplanes to meet the exceptional operational circumstances.

The first requirement was met by the rapid despatch of MR1s from No 42 Squadron to 'hold the air' around Ascension from 6 April 1982 onwards until the MR2s from the Kinloss squadrons, especially those fitted with air-to-air refuelling probes, could arrive and extend the operational radius down to the real scene of the war, some 4,000 miles south. The first of the No 42 Squadron MR1s made their way to Ascension, via Gibraltar, without air-to-air refuelling, under the command of Wg Cdr D.L. Baugh, the OC of No 42 Squadron who remained as Nimrod Detachment Commander until being relieved by the then Wg Cdr (now Group Captain) David Emmerson on 22 April.

The enormous air, sea and land battlefield of the South Atlantic was not entirely strange to old hands in the Nimrod force nor to those who had studied reports of previous exercises. In June 1973 Crew 3 of No 42 Squadron had visited Ascension Island on a goodwill mission and had been duly feted.

It should be remembered that there had been a Parliamentary debate on the Nimrod air-to-air refuelling capability in March 1982 (which has been referred to above), and in April 1982, the month of the invasion and of the sailing of the first Task Force ships, British Aerospace was asked to carry out a feasibility investigation into in-flight refuelling of Nimrods. Since their eventual air-to-air refuelling capability had such a fundamental effect upon the conduct of the war, the following dates and events are of significance:

14 April 1982 An ITP (Instruction to Proceed) on Nimrod AAR (Air-to-Air Refuelling) was received by BAe at Woodford.
18 April Detail drawings complete.

27 April First flight made with equipment in XV229. Dry contacts made with a Victor tanker.
30 April First wet contacts with a Victor.
1 May Nimrod XV238 fitted with AAR delivered to service.
2 May Daylight wet contact released for Service use.
3 May Night wet contact released for Service use.

Instructors in AAR were in short supply at this time, all the experienced tanker crews already being fully occupied at this stage of the war and being primarily concerned with the air-refuelling of the fighters and bombers. Nevertheless, Flt Lt E.L. Banfield, a QFI in this highly specialised field, did valiant work, teaching and checking out 18 Nimrod pilots during 24 sorties.

The theoretical range of an AAR-equipped Nimrod is of the order of some 12,000 miles. Its endurance is not limitless, because other fluids, such as lubricating oils, have to be topped up; and with all the comforts in the world the matter of crew fatigue still has to be taken into account. In very broad terms, given the availability of tankers at the right place and the right time, a Nimrod, like almost any other type of multi-crew aircraft with an AAR probe, can stay airborne reasonably happily for some 24 hours.

The Nimrod presence during the Falklands war built up from the first hastily despatched MR1s of No 42 Squadron to an average strength of four MR2s on any given day. The continuing arrival of MR2s with AAR probes meant that the aircraft's influence on the proceedings gradually spread out from the Ascension Island patrols of about 400 miles radius to the very long sorties to the Falklands themselves, and beyond. The growing list of tasks included the flying of SAR top cover for the RAF Harriers being flown south on to HMS *Hermes* and very importantly the cover and assistance-to-rendezvous for the 'Black Buck' Vulcan bombers with their Victor and Hercules tankers.

Inevitably there were some dramas; many records were claimed and earned. Perhaps the most important record of all was that no casualties were sustained by the Nimrod detachment, nor did any of the 'clients' they were looking after meet with natural disaster over that huge and featureless expanse of ocean.

Among the dramas there was the occasion on 12 May when a Nimrod of No 201 Squadron had a visual sighting of an Argentinian maritime reconnaissance Boeing 707. Sgt Paul Warrener has described to the author the details of this episode and of the sortie which led up to it. Here is his account:

'Number 201 Squadron's first truly operational flight in a theatre of war took place on 12 May 1982. The flight was planned to take off at 06.00 and was due to last 15 hours. The flight would be supported by two waves of Victor tankers.

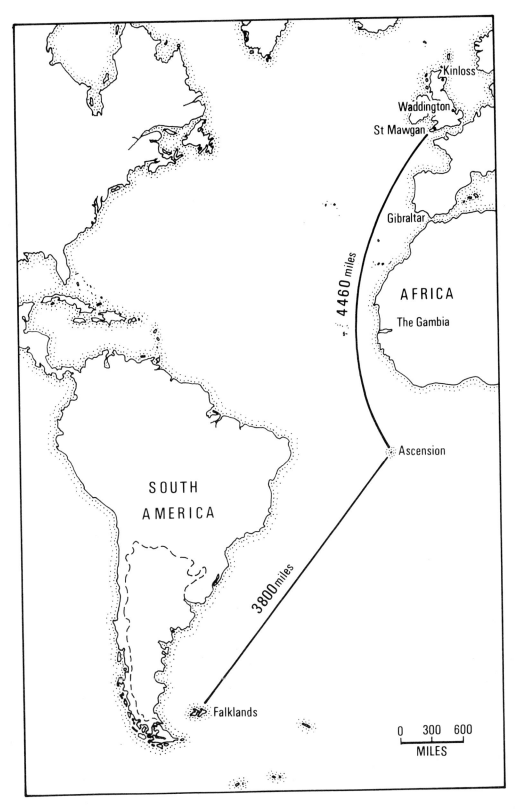

Kinloss

Waddington
St Mawgan

Gibraltar

4460 miles

AFRICA

The Gambia

SOUTH
AMERICA

Ascension

3800 miles

Falklands

0   300   600
MILES

'Because of the distances involved two 'prods' (receptions of fuel from a tanker) would be required. Two waves of five or six tankers would be required. A wave of Victors worked like a reverse avalanche.

'A wave of six would work initially as three pairs and after a certain distance from Wideawake (Ascension) one of the pair would transfer fuel to the other, thus leaving three full tankers. One of these three would then transfer to the other two. Eventually two reasonably full aircraft were left and then one would transfer to the other, leaving *one* full tanker.

'Enter the Nimrod which would take enough to fill its tanks leaving the last Victor with enough to return to Ascension.

'The object of this mission was to provide surface surveillance for Task Force units in transit South to the Falklands.

'After briefing at our own Nimrod Operations HQ (a blue American school bus which judging by its age could have taken Ronald Reagan to school) the crew went to 'Victor Operations' in a tent where air-conditioning could be adjusted by opening or lowering flaps.

'Due to the hostility of the South Atlantic weather Nimrod crews carried "quick-don" immersion suits which had to be worn beyond 35 degress south.

'Whilst heading south the organisation of the "dry" team (responsible for using the sensors used in the surface surveillance) was similar to that of a defence watch. Two sensors required constant monitoring; normal watches of an hour were carried out by the remaining members of the team. After 35 degrees south the crew went to Action Stations with the dry search sensors being manned by the same person while every other member of the rear crew who was not being used on the search sensors would be manning whatever window was spare.

'As we were heading south we detected two aircraft we would normally expect to encounter in the Norwegian Sea, not the South Atlantic. Two "Bear Deltas" were carrying out a normal peacetime mission. The "Bears" were a little bit of a surprise in that when one was looking for Argentinians, a Russian is the last person you are thinking of. You don't find any Argentinians off North Norway!

'Later on in the Flight we detected an Argentinian B 707. The Task Force ships in transit South had already come across a 707 on a few occasions. The first was probably on 21 April when a Harrier of 800 Naval Air Squadron had formated on one.

'At the time of the ESM (Electronic Support Measures) detection on the 707 the environment was fairly quiet. The intercept was classified as only a "Possible" initially with a hint of "Probability" some minutes later. Our aircraft maintained its heading until a bear-

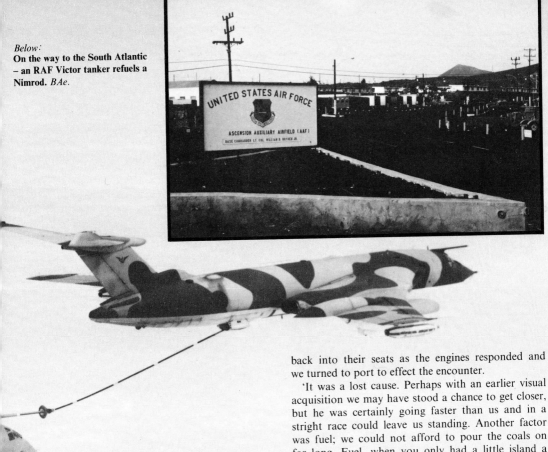

Below:
On the way to the South Atlantic – an RAF Victor tanker refuels a Nimrod. *BAe.*

Left:
No 201 Squadron's pride and joy during the Falklands campaign. Against all official rules this aircraft bore the equivalent of a 'Jane' as might have been displayed on the nose of a Lancaster or a Halifax during World War 2. At Ascension she was variedly referred to as 'Wendy' or 'Jane', depending on the date-stamps on paybooks or those of the holders' fathers. *Sgt Paul Warrener, No 201 Sqn RAF*

Top:
'Concertina City' being built at Wideawake, Ascension. This became home for so many air and ground crews including those of the Nimrod force. The name entered British Forces language because of the structure of the temporary buildings.
Sgt Paul Warrener RAF

ing change was noted and this gave some indication of range.

'The lookouts on the starboard side of the aircraft were straining to see the other aircraft, whilst the port side were a little bit envious of them.

'The Flight Deck got him first. He was at a similar level to us, passing right to left.

'The first pilot pushed the throttles open as we turned to intercept – unarmed. The crew were pushed back into their seats as the engines responded and we turned to port to effect the encounter.

'It was a lost cause. Perhaps with an earlier visual acquisition we may have stood a chance to get closer, but he was certainly going faster than us and in a stright race could leave us standing. Another factor was fuel; we could not afford to pour the coals on for long. Fuel, when you only had a little island a few thousand miles away to land on, was worth more than any other priceless commodity available.

'Had we had Sidewinders (Sgt Warrener's aircraft was not so fitted at that time) the Fleet would have been a little less worried and Nimrod would have added another feather to its cap.'

On 3 June 1982 a Vulcan captained by Sqn Ldr Neil McDougal attacked radar stations at Port Stanley with two of its four Shrike anti-radar missiles in the course of Operation 'Black Buck 6'. On its way back to Ascension four hours later and while attempting to refuel from a Victor off the Brazilian coast its AAR probe was damaged. The tanks were by then almost empty and the nearest airfield was at Rio de Janeiro some 400 miles west.

Sqn Ldr McDougall, who had Flt Lt Brian Gardner aboard as extra pilot and Flt Lt Rod Trevaskus in the back, decided to divert there at the risk of internment, dropped his two remaining Shrikes and descended to low level in order to jettison confidential documents. These papers were packed into a weighted navigator's bag and thrown out as soon as the aircraft could be de-pressurised. It was then discovered that the door could not be closed and it became impossible to climb again to the fuel economy height of about 40,000ft. A full Mayday was transmitted. The door was closed eventually and a rapid landing made at Rio with about 3,000lb of fuel left – insufficient even for one circuit of a strange airfield.

During the crisis a Nimrod acted as 'Good Shepherd', not crossing neutral airspace itself but giving navigational advice to the Vulcan crew who had thrown out most of their charts with the confidential documents. The Nimrod also acted as a long range communications relay station passing diplomatic messages between London, Brazilia and Rio de Janeiro which resulted in the 'correct' treatment of the Vulcan crew and their eventual release together with the aircraft.

As early as 21 April a Nimrod assisted – by providing SAR cover – in the establishment of an RAF long distance reconnaissance record when a Victor tanker of No 55 Squadron, captained by Sqn Ldr John Elliott, supported by three other similar aircraft, took a look (from 18,000ft) at South Georgia on a 7,000-mile mission. The shepherding Nimrod spent 14 hours 45 minutes in the air.

Other notable missions included an AAR-equipped Nimrod flying 2,750 miles SSW of Ascension as anti-submarine cover for the main reinforcement convoy on 11 May and an 8,300-mile, 19-hour 5-minute sortie on 15 May to ensure that the Argentine Navy could not threaten the amphibious landings.

On 20 May the progress of the re-invasion force was watched by a Nimrod of No 206 Squadron with Wg Cdr David Emmerson, by then Commander of the Nimrod Detachment, aboard. The aircraft then flew a long reconnaissance parallel to, and about 60 miles from, the Argentinian coast.

Other relatively mundane tasks included the constant provision of top cover to helicopters and the dropping of mail to surface ships and submarines.

During the rapid progress of the war the 'up-gunning' of the Nimrods went on apace, some of it carried out at Kinloss and St Mawgan, some at Woodford, with final touches made at Ascension. The installation of the Sidewinders, giving the aircraft a self-defence capability, began on 14 May at a feasibility meeting at Woodford, and an Instruction to Proceed (ITP) was issued to British Aerospace.

On 26 May the first flight of XV229 equipped with Sidewinders took place at Woodford and on 28 May the installation was released for Service use. On 31 May XV232 was delivered to Service following its return to Woodford a week earlier and by the end

of June eight aircraft had been modified, six at Woodford and two at Kinloss.

The Harpoon installation programme began on 13 April when BAe also carried out a feasibility study for a Martel fit. A Harpoon bomb-bay installation was decided upon by 28 April and an ITP received on 7 May. The first flight of a Harpoon equipped Nimrod (XV234) took place on 9 June, the first live firing from Boscombe Down being carried out on 11 June. After Release for Service Use was authorised on 12 June, XV237 was delivered to Service on 19 June and XV234 on 24 June. Subsequent aircraft were modified at RAF Kinloss.

As well as the rapid installation of the 'iron bomb' equipment giving the aircraft an air-to-surface ship capability (at least of sorts), Nimrods were loaded with Stingray torpedoes still under test. The stimulus of war had displayed itself in no small way throughout the Nimrod world.

Wideawake Airfield on Ascension, technically an American base which the UK was able to use, offered reasonably comfortable climatic conditions compared with those which had to be endured further South. Nevertheless living conditions were spartan in what became known as 'Concertina City' and much ingenuity required to provide even line servicing for an average of four Nimrods on the base at any time. One of the prides of the Nimrod detachment – which reached a strength of about 150 air and ground crew personnel – was the top-up bowser constructed from an ancient commandeered US vehicle made to run on a combination of aircraft fuel and lubricating oil.

All four Nimrod squadrons sent air and ground detachments to Ascension during the course of the war, No 206 eventually giving all its crews the experience. Individual aircraft came and went according to servicing and modification requirements. All, including the Mk 1s of No 42 Squadron, were painted in the new hemp camouflage scheme.

No aircraft were lost, no one was hurt, much experience was gained, and much pride was taken – and still is taken – in the Nimrods' contribution to the South Atlantic solution, which was somewhat underpublicised at the time.

At the time of publication of this book the NR Nimrods will have completed more than 15 years of service and happily there has been no need to include a separate 'attrition' or crashes and losses chapter. Only one aircraft has been totally lost, and only two aircrew – the pilots of that Mk 2, No XV256 – have lost their lives.

Just before 07.30hrs on 17 November 1980 XV256 took off from Kinloss with 20 souls on board, many of them rear crewmen on the final phase of their conversion course from MR1 to MR2s. Immediately after take-off and at about 20ft altitude the aircraft flew through a dense flock of sea birds. No 1 engine surged violently and Nos 2 and 3 lost thrust. Left with residual power on No 4 engine, which may also have been

damaged, the captain, Flt Lt Noel Anthony of the Royal Australian Air Force, endeavoured to maintain what little height and speed he had by ordering full power on the live engines and raising the undercarriage. However he was soon faced with no alternative but to attempt a controlled crash landing. Some 27 seconds after take-off the aircraft came down on the relatively soft tree tops of a forest area 1,300yd from the end of the runway and was alsmost immediately engulfed in flames. Eighteen crew members managed to evacuate the wreckage but both Flt Lt Anthony and his co-pilot, Flg Off Stephen Belcher RAF, were killed. There were no casualties on the ground and damage was confined to Forestry Commission property.

The investigation established that the cause was a multiple bird strike which occurred at a critical stage of flight and the official report stated:

'The aircraft suffered such a severe loss of thrust that maintenance of height and flying speed quickly became impossible.

'It was the captain's skill in keeping the stricken aircraft airborne long enough to make a very smooth and controlled crash at minimum speed into the tree tops that undoubtedly saved the lives of the 18 crew members.

'After the accident 77 dead sea birds were found on or near the runway. It is not known how many others were ingested by the aircraft engines.'

Flt Lt Anthony was posthumously awarded the Air Force Cross and Flg Off Belcher the Queen's Commendation for Valuable Services in the Air.

A number of additional bird strike precautions were subsequently instituted at Kinloss and the lessons of the accident studied throughout the RAF. Dusk and dawn take-offs, especially during certain wind and tide conditions on the Moray Firth, are now restricted at Kinloss.

At 11.09hrs on 2 June 1984 Nimrod XV257 of 42 Squadron took off from St Mawgan on a TACEVAL (Tactical Evaluation) search and rescue sortie. When outbound checks were called seven miles from base it was discovered that there was a fire in the weapons bay. The captain decided to turn back and he landed on the reciprocal runway. In five minutes after touching down the fire burnt off the clam-shell doors, went through the roof of the bomb bay and filled the rear cabin with smoke. There were no casualties and the Station fire crew – who had been despatched to a distant location as part of the TACEVAL exercise – received a 'Well Done' certificate after their leader, Warrant Officer Allan Quayle, used his own initiative to return without orders.

Damage was limited to about half the weapons bay and the adjacent fuselage structure but the aircraft was eventually flown back to Woodford for Category 4 repair.

4 Search & Rescue and Offshore Tapestry

A one or two line paragraph accompanies most newspaper accounts of dramatic air-sea rescues involving helicopters, lifeboats, warships, merchant ships and Coastguards. It usually just says, 'An RAF Nimrod also took part in the rescue operation.' Behind laconic and brief references lies a vast store of knowledge and experience, the employment of many skills, the use of a very complicated aeroplane, and often the display of much physical endurance and courage.

For many reasons the crews of the Nimrods participating in 'live' Search & Rescue missions and those of their forebears in Shackletons have seldom received their fair share of publicity even after events such as the Fastnet yatch race disaster and the capsizing of the *Alexander Kielland* oil rig.

There are several reasons for this. One is that the maritime reconnaissance squadron bases at Kinloss and St Mawgan are a very long way from even the furthest-flung media bases, and certainly an extremely long way from London where too many decisions about what the public should see and read are still made. Another reason perhaps has been that the Shackletons and Nimrods have often remained airborne and switched to other tasks for long after the helicopters have landed with their crews able, quite rightly, to give interviews and explain the part that the armed forces play in the saving of life.

Air sea rescue, later styled search and rescue, has been the most important secondary role for maritime aircraft from World War 1 onwards. The first fully recorded Air Sea Rescue *attempt* occurred in September 1917 when an RNAS H-12 flying boat alighted in the Eastern half of the North Sea to succour the crew of a DH4 landplane which had ditched shortly after both of them had shot down Zeppelin L44 near the Terschelling Islands. The flying boat did 'alight' and its crew rescued the pilot and observer of the DH4 just before it sank. In the natural laws militating against flying boats in heavy seas (laws which eventually led to the adoption of the landplane and thereby the Nimrod as the most effective form of maritime flying machine) the H-12 could not take off again. All six crew from the two aircraft were eventually rescued, largely through the intervention of a very gallant pigeon which died from exhaustion while trying to deliver its precious position message, but which nevertheless died in the right place. (The details of this historically important ASR episode can be found

in C.F. Snowden Gamble's book *The Story of a North Sea Air Station* and in my summary of the account in *Helicopter Rescue*.)

In the early and middle stages of World War 2, Coastal Command Sunderlands, Catalinas and land-based aircraft made many valiant attempts to rescue aircrew and others from the hostile oceans on which, under which and over which, so much of that war was fought. Sadly not all that many were successful. The aircraft of those days did not, of course, have the sort of searching, nor rescue, equipment as is possessed by the Nimrod force.

Once Coastal Command had settled on the VLR (Very Long Range) landplane as its main instrument of war many such aircraft were specifically allocated to the air sea rescue task and fitted with airborne life-boats designed by Uffa Fox and manufactured by Saunders Roe. A number of medium range Coastal landplanes such as the Lockheed Hudsons were also

fitted with lifeboats. The first generation of immediate postwar Coastal Command VLR landplanes consisted of Mk 3 Lancasters. The first batch were designated Lancaster ASR3s, were equipped with the Saunders Roe lifeboats and had rescue as their primary task. A little later these and other Lancasters were designated GR (General Reconnaissance) Mk 3s and they plugged the gap until the appearance of the Shackleton in 1949 and its entry into service in 1951.

By the early 1950s, however, a superior piece of life-saving equipment, known as Lindholme Gear, had been perfected; this was carried by the majority of Shackletons and is still in use to the present day in Nimrods and in the remaining Airborne Early Warning Shackletons. (Lindholme Gear, like two other sets of life-saving equipment, the Bircham Barrel and the Thornaby Bag, was named after the RAF station where it was invented. The latter two devices, constructed from empty bomb-casings, only had short lives but proved to be reasonably effective means of delivering comforts from an aircraft to survivors fighting for their lives in the sea.)

Lindholme Gear consists of three containers. The large, central, one is an MS9 liferaft, normally capable of succouring nine people or up to 12 in overload conditions. Two smaller containers, attached to the central liferaft by floating ropes, one about 150yd long, the other about 300yd, are packed with stores. The Gear can be dropped from Nimrods (and from Shack-letons, Hercules and other large aircraft) in the form of a stick, with a static line activating the deployment of a restraining parachute. Fairly complicated approach patterns have to be flown at low level to achieve the desirable end-product of the floating ropes virtually wrapping themselves round survivors in the water without them having to make much physical effort to board the central liferaft and draw in the extra containers. Depending upon the relative speed of drift of the Lindholme Gear and that of the survivors, be they in lifeboats, liferafts, clinging to flotsam or perhaps just afloat in lifejackets, a decision has to be made by the aircraft captain as to whether he drops up-wind, downwind, or across-wind. Because the Lindholme Gear containers are provided with drogues which give them a very slow rate of drift they are most often dropped downwind of the survivors who will then be blown on to them (although not always!) The final flight path is usually made across-wind. Sometimes, however, the circumstances would be the other way round – if for example survivors are in a substantial ship's lifeboat streaming a sea anchor. It all calls for nice judgment, particularly if the rescue has to be carried out at night when flares or other forms of illumination may have to be deployed first. Nimrods deploying Lindholme Gear normally also drop a sonobuoy and a smoke float on each pass which can be back-tracked on to.

Although seldom used by Nimrods even in practice, the aircraft can also carry items called CLE (Containers Land Equipment) packed with survival stores which can be dropped by parachute to those in distress on the land.

Until the advent in the UK of medium-radius (200nm) twin-engined S-61 and Sea King rescue helicopters in the 1970s the prime movers in most air-sea rescues at more than 50nm off the coasts were the maritime reconnaissance fixed-wing aircraft, first the Shackletons and then the Nimrods. To a great extent they still have a vital part to play in the short and medium-range rescue tasks since even twin-engine helicopters can get into trouble and like to have top-cover.

The principle search and rescue functions for the four Nimrod MR squadrons (plus occasionally No 236 OCU) are as follows:

The Search element Nimrods, with their comprehensive range of electronic equipment aboard, plus 13 pairs of human eyes, are ideally equipped to find casualties in vast expanses of ocean, be they still aboard a ship in distress, in a lifeboat or a liferaft, or even floating alone in a lifejacket. Having found survivors they then have the ability through their many communications links to home in other rescuers, perhaps helicopters, perhaps lifeboats, perhaps warships or merchant vessels.

The Control element Very often in a complex rescue operation involving many different agencies, the captain of a Nimrod, probably a flight lieutenant in his late 20s, will be in the ideal position to assume the duties of On Scene Commander or Scene of Search

Commander – sitting above it all, with a broad picture of what is going on, able to talk to all concerned, and while perhaps not actually issuing orders to commodores and admirals and the like, certainly in a position to proffer firm advice, which is usually taken without question.

The Long Distance Rescue element Disasters at sea can and do still occur outwith the range of the biggest and best helicopters. As already explained, Nimrods have the capability of giving direct aid to survivors by the dropping of Lindholme Gear.

The SAR stand-by system in the Nimrod force provides for each of the four squadrons to undertake a week's tour of duty involving the provision of one 'scramble' aircraft loaded with two sets of Lindholme Gear and some other special equipment on one hour's readiness for take-off.

In addition of course, there is usually a Nimrod already in the air somewhere in UK airspace which can be diverted from a training task to the scene of a disaster. Such aircraft always have one set of Lindholme Gear loaded in the weapons bay as a matter of routine. (No 8 Squadron's AEW Shackletons also always carry a set of Lindholme in case they happen to be within easy reach of a problem.)

Another important SAR responsibility for the Nimrod squadrons is the provision of cover for Royal and some VIP flights anywhere in the world. This sometimes leads to some welcome overseas deployments. The provision of SAR top cover was an ingredient of the Nimrods' role in the Falklands war as referred to earlier.

The two major rescue incidents which remain in the public mind, and which involved Nimrods, are those of the Fastnet yacht race disaster in August 1979 and of the capsizing of the *Alexander Kielland* oil industry accommodation platform in the North Sea in March 1980. In the case of the first event the Nimrods' ability to carry out radar and visual searches over a vast sea area (about 20,000 square miles) came to the fore. During the Fastnet disaster aircraft from Nos 42 (St Mawgan), 120 and 201 (Kinloss) Squadrons played a vital part in the whole rescue operation. Although

Centre right:
A deployed MS9 dinghy on the trampoline of the trimaran *Bonifacio* which capsized during the 1981 *Observer* Transatlantic race. The drop was made by Flt Lt Ken Deveson and his No 201 Squadron crew. The survivors, Americans Philip Steggall and Thomas Wiggins were later picked up by the MV *Anangel Happiness*. They wrote to the Secretary of State for Defence saying that they were sighted by the Nimrod within two hours of switching on their emergency locator beacon, and commenting: 'From that moment on we were to experience firsthand a co-ordinated rescue that would be a standard for the rest of the world to follow. *RAF*

Right top and bottom:
The stern half of the Greek tanker *Victory*. *RAF*

72

No 42 Squadron was not at the time holding the SAR stand-by responsibility and station block-leave had only just ended, five Nimrod crews were put on immediate stand-by and the normal flying training programme abandoned as soon as the news broke of the immensity of the disaster.

Crew 3 of No 42 Squadron with the CO, Wg Cdr David Green, aboard, and with Flt Lt John Labercombe as Captain, soon sighted among many others in distress, the seven-man crew of the yacht *Gringo* in their liferaft, and were able to home in a Royal Navy Sea King to them, which winched all of them to safety. Mr Richard Milward, *Gringo*'s skipper, later wrote to Wg Cdr Green, saying: 'After seven hours of sitting in our liferaft we were extremely glad to see the aircraft (Nimrod 51) and our morale was much boosted by the presence close by until the Sea King arrived.'

Many other Fastnet yacht crews had equal cause for gratitude to the Nimrods though many of them may not have been directly aware of their good-shepherding presence overhead, often well above the cloud base.

The *Alexander Kielland* disaster, in which 123 people perished and 89 were rescued, provided a classic example of the Nimrods' effectiveness in the On Scene Commander role. A total of six Nimrods, operating in relays from Kinloss, were overhead from within an hour of the first Mayday call until hope for any more survivors was abandoned about 48 hours later. During this period the activities of 20 British and Norwegian helicopters and 80 surface ships had to be co-ordinated by the Nimrod captains and their crews. During the period of 27/28 March 1980 the role of the Nimrod captains as flying air traffic controllers was especially important because in the low visibility obtaining throughout the operation there was serious risk of mid-air collisions between the many rescue helicopters trying to do their best. There was indeed at least one recorded near-miss of 70ft. At one stage a Nimrod captain had to 'rein back' some of the well meaning efforts of small helicopters flying off rigs and ships and limit the work to the Sea Kings of the RAF and the Royal Norwegian Air Force which were equipped with blind-flying aids.

During 15 years of operational service an extensive record has of course been built up of SAR incidents involving Nimrods. Only a selection of them can be recorded in this book, but perhaps each illustrates a particular asset possessed by the Nimrod in the business of saving and preserving human life.

● In September 1977 Mr Enda O'Coineen attempted to cross the Atlantic single handed in a Zodiac inflatable dinghy. He capsized in mid-ocean but was able to initiate a distress message on his small personal locator beacon. He was found after routine search procedures by a Nimrod of No 120 Squadron captained by Flt Lt, later Sqn Ldr, Steve Roncoroni. The Nimrod

Right and below:
The Blue Riband contender *Virgin Atlantic Challenger* struck a submerged object and sank within 100 miles or her goal on 15 August 1985. Arrangements had been made between her owner Richard Branson, her skipper Chay Blyth, and No 42 Squadron at St Mawgan to 'cover' the last 900nm of her voyage as a training exercise. Nimrods of No 42 Squadron first gave assistance – and gained valuable experience – by arranging refuelling rendezvous with merchant ships. On 15 August Sq Ldr Gordon Laing's crew was diverted from a VJ-day flypast at Plymouth in response to the Mayday from Chay Blyth. The 3ft of *Virgin Atlantic Challenger's* bow section remaining afloat was picked up as an intermittent radar contact at a distance of 14nm. At 6nm range a rescue beacon transmission was heard and one hour 18 minutes after the alert had been passed to Sqn Ldr Laing the crew had the liferafts in sight. Four minutes later the Nimrod crew found the banana boat *Geest Bay* and by first circling her and laying a flare path, then establishing radio contact, they guided her to the survivors. The Nimrod crew then homed in SAR helicopters for the final phase of a classic rescue operation. Pictures (both from RAF St Mawgan) show the *Challenger* going well and the crew in their liferafts.

crew dropped Lindholme Gear to him and then homed the Royal Fleet Auxiliary *Stromness* to his position. Mr O'Coineen was rescued, and both dinghies recovered, by the RFA. This was a classic example of the Nimrod's search and pin-pointing capability.

● Another 'pin-pointing' example. On 9 June 1980 M. Jacques Timsit, taking part in the Royal Western/*Observer* single-handed transatlantic yacht race had to take to his liferaft after his 38ft *Motorola* struck a submerged object about 200 miles West of the Scillies. An RAF Sea King was scrambled from Brawdy, Pembrokeshire, in response to his Mayday call which had been relayed via Paris and Plymouth. He was found by Nimrod Crew 4 of No 42 Squadron (St Mawgan) about two hours after the rescue operation began. M. Timsit, 41, was successfully winched from his liferaft by the Sea King which was homed in to him by the Nimrod.

● An illustration of the Nimrod's ability to act as On Scene Commander and to home in other rescuers. On 15 January 1981 a Dutch Atlantique maritime reconnaissance aircraft with a 12-man crew was engaged in shadowing the Soviet carrier *Kiev* and two

'Kresta' class cruisers off the North coast of Scotland. It had to ditch in a 40kt wind, heavy seas and sleet and snow squalls. Two Sea Kings from 819 Naval Air Squadron at Prestwick and another from 'D' Flight No 202 Squadron RAF at Lossiemouth were scrambled, and a No 42 Squadron Nimrod (captained by Flt Lt Charles Montgomery) acted as On Scene Commander. The helicopters were able to home in to beacon signals from the Atlantique's liferafts and were also guided by the Nimrod. Eight of the Dutch crew were winched to safety by the first RN helicopter on the scene, a ninth member by the second Sea King. Three members of the Atlantique crew died, probably from hypothermia while trying to swim from their ditched aircraft to the liferafts.

● The Nimrod's ability to give aid to those in distress in mid-ocean was displayed when on 11 February 1982 the 12,000-ton Greek tanker *Victory* broke in two in mid-Atlantic about 450 miles north of the Azores in 80mph winds and 65ft waves. Fifteen crew members tried to escape in a lifeboat but it broke up on being launched and its occupants were swept away. A further 16 crew remained aboard the 100ft long stern section of the ship. A Belgian ship, the *Potomac*, was the first rescue vessel on the scene and her crew made repeated unsuccessful attempts to throw a line on board the stern half of the *Victory*.

Nimrod XV235 of No 201 Squadron (Kinloss) using call sign Rescue 51, captained by Flt Lt John Martin, the 1st Navigator, and with Crew 6 aboard, scrambled at 04.00hrs and after a 1,000-mile transit found the stern half of *Victory* and made radio contact. Flt Lt Martin first ordered a close search for the 15 men who had attempted to escape in the lifeboat but no trace of them was seen. The aircraft pilots, Sqn Ldr Mackenzie and Flt Lt Cooke, then managed to straddle the stern half of the ship with Lindholme dinghies and survival equipment in spite of severe turbulence affecting their aircraft and enormous seas throwing the vessel about. Regrettably the survivors still aboard the *Victory* seemed unable to recover this equipment and make use of it although they had radioed that they had little food, water or other supplies on board.

Shortly afterwards, smoke began to pour from the Nimrod's navigation equipment. Power supplies to it had to be shut down and the aircraft headed for the Azores, the crew using sun sights and stand-by compasses, and breathing emergency oxygen, as they coped with cross-winds gusting up to 140mph. An American P-3 Orion finally shepherded them into the Lajes base on the Azores.

Meanwhile another Nimrod from No 42 Squadron (St Mawgan) endeavoured to give assistance by dropping rescue gear in such a way that 600yd of line fell between two ships, thus linking the *Victory's* stern half with the British freighter *Manchester Challenger*. Finally two Dutch frigates arrived on the scene and their Lynx helicopters winched 15 men to safety, plus the body of a sixteenth.

Telegrams of thanks were sent by the President of the Hellenic Chamber of Shipping and by the survivors to 18 Group, to Kinloss and to St Mawgan for the part the Nimrods had played in the rescue.

● In March 1982 a Russian 'H-2' class nuclear submarine with a crew of 90 was spotted in obvious distress about 700 miles northeast of Newfoundland by an American P-3 Orion. Nimrods from Kinloss watched the scene for many hours until Russian tugs were seen to appear and take the vessel in tow. This operation was a clear illustration of the internationalism of rescue operations.

● Another example of internationalism occurred on 26 July 1983 a Nimrod of No 201 Squadron (Kinloss) captained by Flt Lt Bob Henry was diverted from a fishery patrol task to go to the assistance of the Spanish trawler *Monte San Alberto* 330nm west of Stornoway. The Nimrod crew located the vessel but had initial communication difficulties because the skipper could not speak English. However it was established that an urgent helicopter lift was needed for a seaman with badly cut legs. As it would have taken the nearest helicopter (a Sea King from Lossiemouth) to the limit of its range even after refuelling in Benbecula, Flt Lt Henry decided to search for a ship in the vicinity which might be able to proffer help. He found the Russian fish factory ship *Irkutsk* and the British motor vessel *Nicola Prosperity* within reasonable reach. As the latter had no medical facilities on board the Nimrod returned to the *Irkutsk* and – again after some language difficulties – established by radio that she had a doctor on board. Flt Lt Henry then diverted both ships to a rendezvous with the *Monte San Alberto*. The Russian ship's doctor transferred to the Spanish vessel and gave the badly injured seaman surgical treatment, including the amputation of a foot.

Later another Nimrod from St Mawgan homed in a very long range Super Jolly Green Giant CH-53 helicopter of the 67th Aerospace Rescue and Recovery Squadron, United States Air Force, from Woodbridge, Suffolk which winched up the seaman and took him to the Southern General Hospital in Glasgow. This episode could be quoted as a classic international interservice, inter-agency, humanitarian mission involving ships at sea, fixed wing and rotary-wing aircraft, all eventually saving the life of one man. Much pride was taken in it afterwards by all concerned.

Above right:
A Nimrod MR 1 of No 201 Squadron with Crew 2 aboard keeping a watchful eye on the disabled Russian 'Hotel' class submarine. *RAF*

Right:
A closer view of the disabled 'Hotel'. *RAF*

An episode where an instrument of war helped in a good cause. In September 1983 the disabled yachtsman, Michael Spring, paralysed from the waist down, was near to the completion of his gallant single-handed voyage to the Azores and back in his 22ft *Coribee* when he became severely distressed by pressure sores aggravated by salt water. He asked for help by radio and a Nimrod of No 42 Squadron (St Mawgan) captained by Sqn Ldr Gordon Laing was able to divert from a routine training exercise to drop medical supplies. He made contact with Michael Spring about 700 miles off Land's End and dropped two containers just 30yd ahead of the yacht.

● At 08.16 BST on Sunday 23 June 1985 the dot representing the Boeing 747 of Air India Flight AI182 with 329 people on board disappeared from the radar screen at Shannon, and RT calls from there to the aircraft were unanswered. At 08.30 the crew of the SAR stand-by Mk 2 Nimrod XV232, provided by No 201 Squadron, Kinloss (captained by Flt Lt Neil Robertson) was put on immediate alert. After the essential consultations between the Shannon Marine Rescue Centre and the British Rescue Co-ordination Centre at Mountbatten, Plymouth, the aircraft was scrambled at 09.08 using callsign 'Rescue 51'. This aircraft was over the last reported position area 100nm southwest of Fastnet (51°N 12°W) in just over an hour and began an Expanding Square search based on a datum point provided by multiple automatic locator beacon signals which proved later to have emanated from liferafts blown clear of the aircraft wreckage. Although the crew had two sets of Lindholme Gear aboard in conformity with the Nimrod SAR stand-by procedure, they only sighted bodies, uninflated liferafts and other flotsam when they made low passes at about 200ft soon after beginning their search pattern. After radioing his sightings, Flt Lt Robertson took on the role of Scene of Search Commander, co-ordinating the activities of helicopters from RAF Brawdy, RNAS Culdrose and USAF Woodbridge plus those of numerous surface ships. Although the weather was fair with a 1,000ft cloud base and a 2–3 sea-state he had to take care that the risk of mid-air collisions between helicopters was eliminated. Some 5½ hours later he was relieved by another No 201 Squadron Nimrod (captained by Sqn Ldr Tony Thomas) and returned to Kinloss to tell reporters: 'There were no signs of life at all. We have all been involved in minor incidents before but not a catastrophe on this scale. It was very sobering.'

Over the next night and day three more No 201 Squadron Nimrods worked on the search task which by then had become one of obtaining evidence for the cause of the disaster rather than in the hope of saving life. A total of four No 201 Squadron Nimrods logged 96 hours 40 minutes; of these 21 hours 30 minutes were while 'on task' in the search area, co-ordinating the efforts of the helicopters and ships recovering bodies, liferafts and small pieces of wreckage

which might eventually provide clues for the accident investigators. There was much sadness throughout all the elements of the British and Irish rescue organisations involved. Both had reacted in copybook manner to one of the world's worst air disasters. Had anyone survived the probable mid-air explosion and then impact with the sea they would undoubtedly have been saved since the water temperatures in the area at the time would have allowed survival for about five hours before hypothermia set in. The efficiency of the Nimrod SAR stand-by procedure earned particular praise from all concerned.

Offshore Tapestry

The codeword Tapestry is a long-standing, Whitehall-coined one referring to all activities by ships, aircraft and some land-based agencies concerned with the protection of British interests in Sovereign Sea Areas, including fishery rights and oil and gas extraction rights.

The choice of the word is believed to have had something to do with the interwoven nature of the many agencies involved – the Royal Navy, the Royal Air Force, the Ministry of Agriculture Fisheries & Food, the Department of Agriculture & Fisheries for Scotland, and the Department of Energy to name but a few.

Although it participated to some extent in earlier years, flying what were then termed Oil Rig Surveillance Patrols (ORSPs) the Nimrod force of No 18 Group really became involved in Tapestry in a big way on the establishment of the 200-mile Exclusive Economic Zone (EEZ) on 1 January 1977. This

arrangement, which fell under European Economic Community regulations, required Britain to police its zone and enforce its rights, although the administration was vested in Brussels. It meant that the UK had sovereign rights over about 270,000 square miles of sea surrounding the British Isles containing oil and gas rigs and fishing grounds in which it had an interest.

Well before the agreement was signed it was assessed that a large share of the enforcement task would fall upon the Nimrods of No 18 Group since they were the most effective aircraft to hand, supported by a complex and efficient back-up system, and perhaps most importantly flown by crews fully competent to handle the work. It was a fairly formidable extra task to unload on to the RAF since it would involve about 180 additional flying hours per month, amounting to 25 sorties, or nearly one per day. Happily as it turned out, four additional Nimrods had become available in 1977 as a result of the political withdrawal from Malta and the disbandment of No 203 Squadron. These aircraft were distributed between the Kinloss and St Mawgan bases, not to become exclusive to 'Tapestry' but to stiffen the overall availability.

The implications of the task were assessed at an early stage and a trial sortie was flown on 8 July 1976 in a Nimrod of No 120 Squadron operating from RAF Machrihanish, with Sqn Ldr David Sames as captain and two Ministry of Agriculture Fisheries & Food officers aboard. Various operating techniques were tested to establish the best methods of locating, identifying and photographing the hundreds of vessels which were fishing in the Irish Sea alone on that day. Photography was obviously going to be a vital part of the whole task and a series of prints, negatives and 'blow-ups' were produced within an hour of landing to enable MAFF specialists to evaluate them. Several further sorties were flown in subsequent weeks. Happily too it also became clear from the outset that the Tapestry operations would fit in well with existing training programmes since many of the techniques of fast transit, searching and finding and then carrying out low-level manoeuvres had much in common with those required for anti-submarine warfare and maritime surveillance tasks. In rather the same way that Search and Rescue helicopter units of the RN and the RAF had for years welcomed the opportunities to deal with live situations rather than practise with oil drums and dummies, the Nimrod force happily took on the Tapestry EEZ responsibility.

Under 'paper-costing' arrangements between government departments the bill for Nimrod Tapestry operations, now running at about £5million a year, is picked up jointly by the MAFF, the DAFS (Department of Agriculture & Fisheries Scotland) and the Department of Energy: it makes no difference in the long run to the taxpayer.

Under the EEZ arrangements there are four fishery patrol areas: these are No 1 extending to west of

ROYAL AIR FORCE STATION
KINLOSS
POWER TO THE HUNTER

SQUADRON
120 120
ROYAL AIR FORCE
ENDURANCE

Below:
Kinloss line. *RAF*

Rockall; No 2 to the north of Shetland; No 3 half-way across the North Sea with the Moray Firth line as its northern boundary and the Wash line as its southern limit; and No 4 running from the Norfolk coast, down the Channel and out into the Western Approaches from Land's End. In general terms the Kinloss squadrons, Nos 120, 201 and 206, accept responsibility for Areas 1, 2 and 3; the St Mawgan units, No 42 Squadron and occasionally No 236 OCU, look after Area 4.

On the fishery side of Tapestry the main task of course is to seek out, look at and photograph every vessel fishing in the Zone, be it British, be it a foreigner licensed to fish or be it an illegal trespasser. The general plan provides for the whole Zone to be covered during the course of a week. At least one Tapestry sortie a day is flown and some 19,000 photographs are taken in an average year.

Numerous suggestions were made in the late 1970s and 1980s that Nimrods were expensive aeroplanes to employ on this sort of task, nevertheless they have always done it efficiently and, under the break-down explained above, in a reasonably cost-effective manner.

On the aspect of the security of oil and gas rigs the main task is to ensure that all such installations of British interest are physically viewed at regular intervals, communication established both by radio and by lamp signal, photographs taken and assurances obtained that nothing untoward has occurred. Even the possibility of a hi-jacking operation does have to be taken seriously and does not just dwell in the realms of adventure fiction.

A typical day for a Nimrod crew allocated to a Tapestry mission (this happens about once a month on average) begins with up to three hours of pre-planning and briefing before an 08.00hrs take-off. The preliminary procedures include the provision of intelligence on likely activities from local fishery inspectors and from officers of MAFF and DSAF permanently resident at St Mawgan and Kinloss, plus an up-date on the licensing arrangements operative on the day – these can vary quite substantially. The resident officers are frequently fliers themselves and their personal knowledge of the size, shape and special characteristics of many hundreds of fishing vessels is of inestimable value to the aircrews.

After transit, Tapestry sorties are usually flown at between 1,000 and 2,000ft depending on cloud base, with descents to much lower levels during the photographic and visual observation passes. Photography is normally carried out at 200ft using the oblique hand-held F134 or F139 cameras, whenever possible through one of the opening windows in the beam. The object is always to obtain a picture clearly showing the vessel's name and number. (By 'Murphy's Law' the vessel being photographed will almost always descend into a wave trough just as the crewman presses his exposure switch.)

If and when 'villains' are found fishing illegally, complicated procedures have to be followed. The first and relatively easy one is to home in a surface fishery protection vessel to carry out an arrest if necessary. There is also a procedure under which the aircraft can issue RT instructions, perhaps laying a line of smoke flares as a course to be followed out of prohibited waters, or even towards a port of arrest.

A claim was in fact made by Crew 7 of No 42 Squadron that it carried out the first Nimrod fishing arrest in 1978 when the captain, Flt Lt Bob Ware, closed up on a Spanish trawler in the Western Approaches. Initial RT contact produced the reply that nobody aboard spoke English but, somewhat to the surprise of the vessel's skipper, Lt Cdr D. Beaugureau, United States Navy, attached Royal Air Force, spoke to him in impeccable Spanish and suggested he proceeded forthwith to Milford Haven, which he did.

A very complicated legal process under the mysterious code-name of 'Belenos' has to be followed if a Nimrod crew is to bring legal action on its own. This involves the production of timed, dated and certified photographic prints and the presence of aircrew in court to give sworn evidence.

Tapestry missions are generally enjoyed by aircrews and they frequently attract guests on board, from Cabinet Ministers to adventurous journalists. They are, however, frequently trying to the constitution, often involving eight or so hours low level flying in turbulence with much energetic manoeuvring.

The Nimrod force also participated in the Icelandic Cod Wars of 1972–73 and 1975–76, with aircraft from all four squadrons flying eight-hour sorties in support of the Royal Navy surface vessels. As late as 1983 Nimrods also mounted a watch, and provided a certain deterrent effect, upon Danish fishing vessels threatening UK limits during the controversy of that year.

Watching for oil slicks or watching for almost anything untoward at sea constitutes a constant part of the Nimrods' 'non-belligerent' activities. Various newspaper reports have indicated down the years that they have played their part in the apprehension of other miscreants at sea, but for many sensible reasons details of these activities have usually been discreetly veiled. In the same way that the very presence of a Sunderland or a Halifax overhead curtailed the activities of enemy U-boats in World War 2 the sight and sound of a Nimrod at low level can concentrate the mind of a smuggler of anything from drugs to arms, quite wonderfully.

5 The Saga of the AEW Mk 3

In a loose sense the phrase airborne early warning can be taken to mean the prime function of any flying machine in the reconnaissance role, from that performed by balloons and man-lifting kites onwards. Since World War 2 however, and more specifically since the Japanese attack on Pearl Harbour in 1941, it has meant the detection of incoming aircraft or missiles flying below the horizons of ground or ship based radar stations. In simple terms the modern airborne early warning aircraft is a flying radar station with the benison of instantly adjustable height to extend the set's range over the curvature of the earth to the limit of its transmission and receiving power. Most AEW aircraft have the further role of becoming flying fighter control stations once enemies have been detected.

Pearl Harbour led to a crash programme in the United States under the code name 'Cadillac' and to the evolution of the AN/APS 20 airborne radar, still in use to this day in No 8 Squadron's Shackletons in the 'Foxtrot Improved' version.

For some 30 years AEW was primarily the concern of the navies of the Western world, the protection of ships both in harbour and at sea being of especial importance. Latterly the division of responsibility for the art between navies and air forces has become blurred as the technique of very low flying by attack aircraft of all types and the growing use of unmanned weapon carriers (missiles) have dominated air strategy, both over land and sea.

By the end of World War 2 the United States Navy was deploying carrier-borne Grumman TBM-3W Avengers in the AEW role although they were not worked up in time to influence the great Pacific sea battles involving the Japanese Kamikaze attacks. The Royal Navy acquired a fleet of Douglas AD-4 Skyraiders in 1952 under the Mutual Defence Assistance Programme and later adopted the Fairey Gannet Mk 3 as its own mount for AN/APS 20 radars. Forty-four Gannet AEW Mk 3s were built and went into service in 1960 with their double-Mamba contra-rotating turboprop power units and complex wing-folding systems. The last of them remained operational until the last 'conventional' carrier, the previous HMS *Ark Royal*, paid off in November 1978. Her de-commissioning and the disbandment of No 849 Naval Air Squadron which flew her Gannets left a serious gap in the Fleet's indigenous air defence cover which was dramatically and tragically exposed during the Falklands war, various proposals to 'plug' it having been earlier rejected on so-called economy grounds.

When the decision was made in the late 1960s to phase out the conventional fixed-wing carriers from the Royal Navy there were reasonable grounds to suppose (although they were questioned in many farther-sighted quarters) that the Royal Air Force would be able to provide AEW cover for the Fleet from land bases, at least in Northern waters, as well as for the defence of the United Kingdom. At least two potent

Below:
The hasty airborne early warning solution at the end of the Falklands war – a Mk 2 Sea King carrying a Searchwater radar in a retractable dome partly made out of British Gas piping and spare undercarriage hydraulic items.
Westland Helicopters

Above:
Nimrod AEW3 XZ286 in flight, displaying the proportions of the tail radome. *BAe*

long-range land-based AEW aircraft were coming on offer; these were the American Boeing E-3A Sentry (AWACS) or an indigenous Nimrod variant. One or the other, RAF chiefs thought, should be in their hands by the late 1970s at most and there was an 'interim solution' (to be described in detail later) available.

During the early and middle 1970s the Labour-controlled HM Governments of the day mulled over the pros and cons of the American and British alternatives with all the factors of UK employment and time-scales to take into account. By this time it had become clear too through NATO intelligence that the Warsaw Pact countries were developing fighter bombers capable of mounting low-level, high-speed attacks on Western Europe and the UK. The whole matter of AEW had become a European one. Both programmes had their attractions. The AWACS (Airborne Early Warn-

ing & Control System) mounted in the well-proven Boeing 707 airframe had reached an advanced stage of development, and was on offer to NATO for the formation of a multi-national AEW force.

The NATO defence ministers sat in conclave on many occasions to discuss the formation of an AEW force. These talks ran into some very complicated politicking with West Germany's representatives often holding back from some of the proposals for the multinational unit.

During this period of prevarication, HM Government, with Mr Fred Mulley as Secretary of State for Defence, finally came down in favour of the Nimrod AEW3 project, not only as the British nation's own defender but as an eventual contributor to any forthcoming multi-national NATO force. A formal announcement to this effect was made on 31 March 1977.

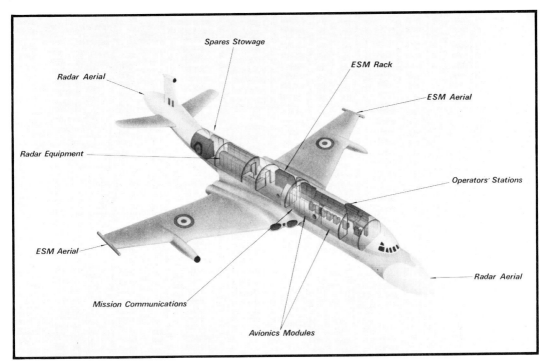

Spares Stowage
ESM Rack
Radar Aerial
ESM Aerial
Radar Equipment
Operators' Stations
ESM Aerial
Radar Aerial
Mission Communications
Avionics Modules

Above left:
A ground mock-up of the Nimrod AEW3 sensor positions.
Marconi Avionics

Left:
The AEW Nimrod multi-function consoles are the equipments which allow AEW operators to 'interface' with the whole of the Mission System Avionics (MSA). This picture shows the testing of consoles under manufacture. *Marconi Avionics*

Meanwhile, the British interim solution or temporary expedient had been launched five years earlier to provide some sort of AEW cover for the Fleet, at least in Northern Atlantic waters around the Iceland–Faroes–Shetland 'Gap', and for the UK Defence System over the North Sea. It consisted of the re-formation of No 8 Squadron RAF, a former fighter unit with a distinguished record, and equipping it with 12 Mk 2 Shackletons which still had plenty of airframe life. This interim solution or temporary expedient was to go on a lot longer than anticipated and survived into 1985 and beyond in spite of a Conservative Government cut (ordered by Mr John Nott as Secretary of State for Defence) in 1981 reducing the aircraft strength from 12 to six.

No 8 Squadron went valiantly on with five Shackletons (one having had to be placed in reserve) while the Nimrod 3 technical problems were still being resolved in the 1980s. Their radars were of course still the faithful AN/APS 20s; the whole Squadron still had a very special spirit about it, perhaps born out of adver-

sity, but patience was beginning to run down as the delays over Nimrod 3 went on, and on. Still no firm date was in sight by the end of 1985.

The airframe design changes from the MR Nimrods to the AEW3s were from the start the obvious ones involving the addition of large bulbous radomes to nose and tail to house the 180°-each fore-and-aft radar scanners, designed by Marconi in contrast to the round-the clock arrangement in the dorsal rotodome of the Boeing AWACS. Originally it was hoped that both the Mk 3 radomes would be of the same size and shape but the nose unit had to be profiled sharply to cope with bird-strike and rain-erosion eventualities as well as presenting a clean aerodynamic entry. Putting the same shape on the tail would have led to an unstable breakaway airflow so a more rounded configuration at the back end had to be adopted. The positioning of both radomes was governed to some extent by the necessity for ground clearance. Perhaps surprisingly the large additions to the noses and tails of the Mk 3 conversions had a beneficial, rather than adverse, effect on directional stability. This was partly because the thicker rear fuselage shape added to the total keel area aft and because it raised the original fin area.

Another feature distinguishing the first Mk 3s to be seen publicly was the addition of ESM pods on the wing tips. These items also began to appear on MR2s from 1984 onwards. The in-flight refuelling systems which had been installed on MR2 aircraft during the Falklands conflict were also embodied on the Mk 3 aircraft.

Above:

To prove the AEW communications system in the Nimrod AEW3 a Transportable Ground Station (TGS) was designed and equipped to co-operate with the AEW Communications Trials aircraft: the equipment in the TGS parallels that in an AEW Nimrod. Monitoring equipment checks and records trials results. *GEC-Marconi Electronics*

Above right:

The AEW Nimrod Mission System Avionics integration rig. This ground rig is a close representation of the aircraft, and is equipped with cabling and cooling to match the aircraft's environment. *GEC-Marconi Electronics*

Test pilots reported at an early stage that the Mk 3 had even better directional stability than that of the MR aircraft. The AEW3s are not, of course, subject to the de-stabilising effect of open bomb-bay doors.

Usually referred to under the collective description 'Mission System Avionics', much of the internal fit of the Mk 3s, developed by Marconi Avionics Ltd (later GEC Avionics) remained classified up to the time of writing, but the following descriptions have been published.

The internal fit of a Nimrod 3 contains three main sensors to detect and classify targets – a multi-mode radar, a passive radio and radar detection system (ESM) and an IFF system to identify friendly targets. The radar passes target plots in terms of range, azimuth, radial velocity and height, to the data handling system. There the information is collated and coordinated with data from the aircraft navigation system, and with further target data from the IFF and the ESM systems. All the information held by the central data processing system can be selected as required by operators for display on their multi-function consoles.

The radar is a multi-mode pulse doppler system which utilises the changed frequency of reflections from moving targets (the doppler effect) to enable low-flying aircraft to be detected even in the presence of strong ground or sea returns.

A statement issued by Marconi in 1980 claimed that the chosen radar frequencies ensured good long range performance and freedom from interference with other existing systems. To cater for modern electronic warfare techniques the system was said to have highly sophisticated anti-jamming devices.

MISSION SYSTEM AVIONICS

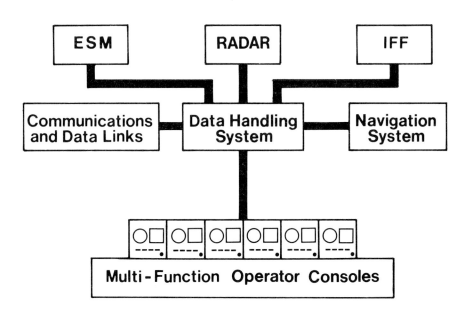

Below:

AEW3 XZ286 in flight. *BAe*

Bottom:

Mission System Avionics production rigs at GEC-Marconi's Hemel Hempstead factory. *GEC-Marconi*

Right:

Internal view of the AEW Communications System ground rig built at the GEC-Marconi Basildon factory to facilitate the electronic, mechanical and ergonomic design of the system. *GEC-Marconi*

The Nimrod 3 is known to carry an extensive communications facility including LF, HF, VHF and UHF; plus radio teletype and data link equipment, all enabling the aircraft to communicate with the ground, with ships, fighters and other AEW aircraft in all foreseeable circumstances.

Other changes noted between the layout of the MR Nimrods and that of the Mk 3s include the fact that as weapons do not have to be carried, bomb bay space can be used for fuel, thereby giving the aircraft a total endurance of well above the normal 12 hours, but not so far specified exactly. Space in the bomb bay is also available for heat exchangers. Since refuelling probes were fitted as standard at a later stage of the conversion programme the endurance can be regarded as probably being well over 24 hours when necessary.

The radar was designed from the outset to be especially effective over water but it has been claimed that it also has as good an overland capability as that of the Boeing Sentry thus making the aircraft compatible with those of the NATO force and of the USAF. Under the fore-and-aft arrangement each radar antenna makes a 180° active sweep followed by a 'dead' return. The movements are synchronised to provide the overall 360° cover. The antennae are about 8ft wide and 6ft high and are stabilised in pitch and roll by gyro platforms.

The data handling system which uses high-speed computer processing to handle returns from all the sensors provides for the automatic tracking of targets. From the computer store, pictures illustrating all the relevant data are displayed at the operator stations for monitoring, and the same information can be transmitted to the ground through the aircraft communication channels for further checking and long-term storage.

The projected crew for the Nimrod 3 is 13 – two pilots, a Flight Engineer, a Routine Navigator and a nine-man mission crew.

The electrical system has had to be up-rated and revised to cope with the very large power demands. Another important consideration has been the provision of adequate cooling for the mass of avionics. A liquid cooling system with final heat transfer to the fuel in the wing tanks has been adopted. Some components are immersed in water-glycol and others cooled indirectly by metal to liquid heat exchangers called cold plates.

Since external radiators would have been too large and would have created enormous drag the expedient of using the wings themselves as 'low-drag radiators' was decided upon. The system takes heat from the fluorocarbon cooling liquid and from the water glycol and transfers it to the fuel in the main wing tanks from where it is dissipated to the air. The standard Nimrod fuel scheduling procedure results in the outer wing tanks being the last to empty so that the 'radiators' remain effective to the end of the on-task portion of the flight.

The Boeing Sentry operates on very different principles. Although its 'chassis' (like that of Nimrod) is that of a proven commercial airliner design the 360° sweep of its radar is provided by the attachment of the mushroom-shaped 'rotodome' above the fuselage. Fairly early information releases claimed that the Sentry's radar range extended beyond 250 miles at 30,000ft. Its rotodome measures 30ft in diameter and the scanner inside it rotates every 10 seconds. At one stage a Comet/Nimrod airframe carrying a Sentry type rotodome was contemplated, and drawings are extant of a multi-role aircraft in this configuration also performing as a tanker. The final chapter of this book will show that such a concept was not all that outlandish.

The Air Staff Target for an Airborne Early Warning Aircraft was issued in August 1972. Following design feasibility studies the Air Staff Requirement was issued in February 1975. A decision was then taken, in advance of a formal go-ahead for the project, to modify a Comet Aircraft to embody a partial Mission System Avionics (MSA) fit.

An early development radar was installed in the fuselage and a representative radome built on to the nose of the Comet. 'One-off' electrical generating, and cooling systems were installed to support the radar. This ungainly aircraft which had begun life as G-APDS with BOAC was designated XW626 and began flight trials at Woodford in June 1977. Trials continued until mid-1980 when the aircraft was transferred to RSRE at Bedford for further experimental work. By the time of writing it had been grounded with no known future.

The formal Instruction to Proceed with the project was given by the Ministry of Defence Procurement Executive in April 1977. A total of 11 AEW Mk 3 aircraft were to be produced. The first three, XZ286, XZ287 and XZ281, were to be used as development aircraft – prior to later refurbishment to full production standard – the remainder to be built as production aircraft for delivery to the RAF.

The development activities on the three aircraft were also to be supported by comprehensive rig installations at Marconi and at BAe Woodford.

The first development aircraft flew from Woodford on 16 July 1980. This aircraft was not equipped with the Mission System Avionics (MSA) and was allocated for airframe performance and handling trials, and the development of the engineering systems required to support the MSA. It was later joined on flight trials by XZ287 in January 1981 and by XZ281 in July 1981, both of these aircraft being allocated for the development and clearance of the Marconi MSA.

Right:
XW626 in flight. *BAe*

Below and bottom:
The roll-out of XZ286, the first development Nimrod AEW3, at Woodford on 30 April 1980. *BAe*

Right:
The tactical operators' station on the AEW3. *BAe.*

In July 1980 XZ286 made its first flight from Wood-ford piloted by Mr Charles Masefield, the BAe Manchester Division Chief Test Pilot, with Mr John Cruise, Nimrod AEW Project Pilot in the second seat, and a crew of four. The aircraft was airborne for $3\frac{1}{2}$ hours, exploring the flight envelope up to 25,000ft.

Afterwards Mr Masefield went on record to say: 'It was a most satisfactory flight. The pre-planned programme was fully completed and the aircraft was found to be extremely stable in the flight region we explored.'

The official company press statement added somewhat emphatically: 'Two other Nimrod AEW aircraft will join the development programme later this year (1980) and early in 1981, leading to entry into service with the Royal Air Force in *early 1982*' (author's italics). Numerous confident statements and glossy handouts were issued in 1980 promising that the Nimrod 3s would be taking their place in the whole NATO AEW system in a couple of years.

Meanwhile No 8 Squadron at Lossiemouth went on valiantly flying and maintaining its last six faithful Mk 2 AEW Shackletons, all concerned confident that it would only be a matter of months before most of them would be transferred to the projected AEW base at Waddington; they would then be re-united with their wives and children on a permanent posting basis and actually move out of their anachronistic flying world into that of the very latest and best in high technology.

Signs that things were going agley began to appear in early 1982 and continued to show themselves up to the middle of 1984. The Squadron received a series of invitations to go on flying its Shackletons 'a bit longer yet', then a new CO and a new QFI were appointed, followed by the posting-in of a number of young aircrew who had to convert from jets to piston-props.

At the turn of 1984–85 it was clear that something fairly serious had gone wrong.

An indication of the profundity of the problem was given both to the RAF and to the general public in January 1985 in the form of brief, non-attributable stories in all national newspapers and on television to the effect that there might be a further *two-year* delay in the programme. It did not take much perspicacity to trace those reports to a deliberate 'leak' from on high and the following month Air Chief Marshal Sir John Rogers, Controller of Aircraft for the RAF, was placed on record in an answer to the House of Commons Defence Committee as saying that the costing of the Nimrod 3 development programme had reached £980million. According to a *Times* report Sir John said that before the decision to develop the Nimrod 3 was taken the Labour Government of the time would have preferred to have entered the NATO project and bought the Boeing AWACS but NATO had 'not been able to get its act together'. Throughout this period of the early part of 1985 the popular press and television made little attempt to differentiate

between the delays attributable to the BAe airframe build and the Marconi MSA build and development. In fact BAe, which was committed to a fixed price contract, produced the Mk 3 airframes significantly in advance of the availability of the MSA equipments. There was negligible delay due to airframe development problems and some recovery was achieved following periods of industrial unrest in 1977 and 1979.

During the 1983–85 period the Royal Air Force went ahead with the establishment of its own AEW force headquarters at the former bomber base of Waddington in Lincolnshire, only recently vacated by the last of the Vulcans. There it assembled ground crews and the beginnings of the large technical back-up organisation clearly required for Nimrod 3 operations. Photographs of a Nimrod 3 were also used in recruiting advertisements for technicians.

In late 1984 the first production AEW Mk 3, XZ285, was transferred from Woodford to RAF Waddington to become the first aircraft of the Joint Trials Unit. This unit, operated jointly by Ministry of Defence Procurement Executive (MODPE) and the RAF, was established to assess the servicing and functioning of the AEW Mk 3 in a Service environment – as distinct from a contractor's trials environment – and to establish the required servicing and training techniques prior to the introduction to squadron use. At this stage it was still not known whether the RAF's Nimrod 3 force would be operated by No 8 Squadron or whether another title would be resurrected.

The general feeling within the RAF was that it would be a travesty of justice if No 8 Squadron was not allowed to carry its number into the new organisation in view of the effort its ground and air crews had put into the task of keeping the Shackletons flying so efficiently.

During all this long 'meantime' the NATO AEW force, equipped with 18 Boeing E-3A Sentries (AWACS) had been formed up and was operating from Geilenkirchen, near Dortmund, West Germany, with its RAF element consisting only of people, and not actual aeroplanes.

As a date check-back it can be recorded that the first standard configuration Boeing E-3A was delivered to the United States Air Force in December 1981. The NATO AEW force took delivery of its first production E-3A in January 1982.

So the matter stood in the summer of 1985, doubts still being cast over the operational efficiency of the

Above right:
WX626 with a 'representative' nose radome but no tail radome, flying from Woodford in 1977. *BAe*

Right:
AEW3 XZ286 taking off on its first flight from Woodford in 1981. *BAe*

Nimrod 3 system, and some senior people with large cheque books around Westminster and Whitehall rightly reluctant to sign one, at a going rate of about £100million per aeroplane, until everyone was satisfied that they were working properly.

A little earlier there had also been the matter of a potential Saudi-Arabian order for AEW aircraft. In 1981 it was reported that the Saudis were definitely interested in the purchase of Nimrod 3s as an alternative to Boeing Sentries. For many reasons the die was cast in the American direction.

Perhaps one reason why the delay and cost-escalation of the Nimrod 3 programme did not reach the proportions of a national scandal in early 1985 was that the decision to follow the go-it-alone AEW course had been taken by a previous Labour Government. When the problems about Nimrod 3 were exposed in early 1985, Opposition spokesmen in the House of Commons seemed to choose to remain silent.

The general public was alerted to the Nimrod 3 programme problems in a BBC *Panorama* programme in February 1985. In the programme and a subsequent article in *The Listener* the presenter, Mr Tom Mangold, questioned the correctness of the original go-it-alone British decision on the Nimrod 3, vis-a-vis the alternative purchase of Boeing AWACS, especially on cost grounds.

In his *Listener* article Mr Mangold put the question: 'If we had played our cards right we could now have full AEW coverage in Britain for a mere £460million. Instead, if we are lucky, we may just get a sort of compromise cover in the next two years at the incredible cost of £1.1billion. Why?'

The programme also displayed to cognoscenti the difference between the original Nimrod MR contracts under which Hawker Siddeley was made the prime contractor on a fixed-price basis and the arrangements for Nimrod 3 conversion programme with Marconi on a cost-plus deal and neither that company or BAe pinned down as a prime contractor.

The *Panorama* programme and the *Listener* article suggested that many serious problems remained in making the whole system work properly, including speculation that the main GEC 4080 computer was overloaded, that the radar transmitters were defective and that another £400million to £500million would have to be expended by Mr Heseltine's Defence Department to make the whole thing work properly even in another two years.

No overt challenges were made against the Panorama programme nor against Mr Mangold's *Listener* article but hopes of better news were expressed to this writer by GEC (Marconi) spokesmen towards the middle of 1985.

At the turn of the year (1985–86) several meetings took place between representatives of the MOD and of GEC. Mr Heseltine, Secretary of State for Defence and Mr Prior the chairman of GEC were present on at least one ocassion. No final decision had been

Below and right:
XZ286 at Woodford. *BAe*

Below:
The tail radome of XZ286, with XV147 behind. *BAe*

Right:
Mr Charles Masefield, at the time BAe Manchester's chief test pilot, just before the take-off of XZ286's first flight on 16 July 1980. *BAe*

Bottom:
XZ286 landing at Woodford. *BAe*

announced however, up to the time of writing in January 1986. At that period of course, the Government and the aircraft industry were 'locked in combat' over the Westland Helicopters affair so the preservation of some silence over the Nimrod 3 matter may have been thought to be judicious on all sides.

Speculation about the Nimrod 3 programme ran fairly rife in early 1985, even in the columns of quite learned aviation journals. Suggestions ranged from the whole programme being abandoned and the Mk 3s being re-converted to MR2s, of which No 18 Group RAF was undoubtedly short; to the whole GEC/Marconi system being put into a bigger airframe such as an Airbus; or Britain buying its way back into the NATO AEW force via the belated purchase of some Sentries.

The speculation went on throughout the year, one report (in *The Sunday Times*) suggesting that the total cost had reached £1.5 Billion and that RAF flying had had to be cut to help pay for the project. This report also quoted a Marconi spokesman as saying that the RAF had regularly altered the Staff Requirement to meet the changing threat from the Warsaw Pact countries.

It was also announced at the Paris Air Show that an arrangement had been reached with Lockheed to fit the GEC-Marconi MSA (Mission System Avionics) into C-130 Hercules with a delivery date for interested customers from 1989 onwards. This announcement led to some speculation that the problems of Nimrod 3 could be associated with the airframe fuselage being too small, or of the wrong shape, to accommodate the MSA, and that the decision to convert 11 MR1 Nimrods in the first place was an unwise, cost-pruning expedient.

The position was clarified to some extent in the autumn of 1985 when non-attributable, but obviously officially inspired, reports appeared in national newspapers, some under the names of Mr Rodney Cowton, the Defence Correspondent of *The Times* and Air

Below:
The 'business back-end' of a Nimrod AEW3 under test at Woodford. *BAe*

Below right:
The AEW3 conversion line at Woodford. *BAe*

Commodore G.S. Cooper, the Air Correspondent of the *Daily Telegraph*. In late August Mr Cowton hinted that a new, fixed-price, contract was being sought between the Ministry of Defence and GEC Avionics to be agreed by the end of the year. His report said that Mr John Lehman, United States Navy Secretary, had recently told British journalists that he was concerned about the delay in introducing Nimrod 3 because NATO counted on it as part of the web of command and control in the North Atlantic.

The possibility of a 're-coup' was discussed in many articles in the lay and technical press with suggestions that the whole Nimrod 3 project might be abandoned and the 11 aircraft involved re-converted to the Maritime Reconnaissance role, with perhaps purchases made of Boeing AWACS Sentries or variants of E-2C Hawkeye used by the USN from carriers in the AEW role.

There was, however, no official support for the latter conjectures and in October 1985 there was some further clarification in the form of another non-attributable news release. This said that the RAF might accept Nimrod 3s with an MSA performance some 25% below expectation, the gap to be closed at a later

stage. It still pointed at 1988 however as the likely year for entry into service even in its less-than-optimum form. It was also suggested in these reports that a completely new computer might be needed, with three times the capacity of that fitted so far, to cope with the aircraft's full operational tasks in the 1990s.

During all this an extensive programme of ground and flight testing was going on at Woodford and RAF Waddington. The programme involved Development Batch aircraft DB2 (XZ287) and DB3 (XZ281) and the first production aircraft P1 (XZ285). DB2 and DB3 were operated from Woodford by BAe and GEC Avionics, frequently carrying MoD(PE) Establishments' specialists, and P1 was operated by the Joint Trials Unit (JTU) established at RAF Waddington.

Of the rest of the 11 aircraft involved in the programme, production aircraft P4 (XZ283) was delivered from Woodford to RAF Waddington in November 1985 and P3 (XV263) was forecast to be delivered at the turn of the year. At the end of 1985 P5 (XZ280) and Development Batch aircraft DB1 (XZ286) were being equipped with their MSAs at Woodford. The remaining aircraft P2 (XV259), P6 (XZ282), P7 (XV262) and P8 (XV261) were effectively complete

as Air Vehicles and were awaiting allocations of GEC Avionics MSAs. However these allocations were dependent upon the outcome of the previously mentioned contractual negotiations between the Ministry of Defence and GEC Avionics.

Meanwhile of course, something had to be done about the Shackletons — the last six of the 'Lovely Old Beasts' were still maintaining a form of NATO AEW cover in the loving hands of all ranks of No 8 Squadron at Lossiemouth. The news releases towards the end of 1985 indicated that the Shacks would have to go on flying well beyond their proud expectation of 35 years front-line service, perhaps to 37 years, or very nearly 40 years from the first test flight. A programme for another set of 'Majors' was initiated for the Shackletons in late 1985, one of the six already having been taken out of service for this purpose and work started at Lossiemouth by the Squadron's own engineers with assistance from a BAe civilian working party and some technicians from Kinloss. Tenders were put out for contract work on the other five aircraft, presumably one at a time, leaving five of these venerable aeroplanes with their dedicated ground and air crews at least plugging the gap in Britain's contribution to the Airborne Early Warning coverage, especially over the vital Faroes Gap.

It would be quite wrong to approach the end of this book about Nimrod on a sour note. I would like to reiterate that the problems associated with the AEW Mk3 version of Nimrod have nothing to do with the design or construction of an aeroplane which has served the nation well for 15 years and will probably continue to do so for at least another 15. In the view of the Royal Air Force — and that means the members of that Service who fly it and maintain it — Nimrod is a superb aeroplane. It remains a pity, at the time of writing, that its name has been associated in the public mind with an expensive problem. By the time this book appears that problem could have been solved, and there is a saying: 'Hindsight is a very fine thing'.

Top left:
An artist's impression of the second Nimrod AEW3 (XZ287) in flight. *BAe*

Bottom left:
A mock-up of the Tactical Area of an AEW3 Nimrod. This picture shows a tactical crew exercising the system in the integration rig. *GEC-Marconi Electronics*

Below:
XZ287, the second Nimrod AEW3, about to take off on its maiden flight from Woodford on 23 January 1981, within 11 days of a scheduled date set nearly three years previously. The flight lasted two hours 45 minutes and went as planned so that there was no need for a second handling flight before going on to the next phase of the programme. *BAe*

6 What Next?

Although the original predictions provided for Nimrod to remain in service until the late 1990s, thought was obviously having to be given to a successor at the time of writing this book. Very careful studies indeed were being made of the ultimate fatigue life of the MR Nimrods, which because of the nature of their business, have been, and still are, subject to much higher flying stresses and corrosion risks than were ever envisaged for the Comet airliner. Within the RAF there was general satisfaction in the mid-1980s with the capabilities of the Nimrod MR 2s, especially since their potential had been extended so much by the modifications made during the Falklands War – the air-to-air refuelling probes and the defensive Sidewinder armament being perhaps the most important additions. The life-span of the AEW Mk 3s, modified from airframes which had consumed little of their predicted fatigue life either in their Mk 1 configuration (while being used by No 203 Squadron from Malta) or as development aircraft, was obviously going to take them well into the 21st century.

The whole subject of future maritime reconnaissance aircraft remained an open one in the West in the mid-1980s, various schools of thought turning towards smaller, cheaper aeroplanes and more of them, or to larger multi-role types with even greater endurance and perhaps carrying slip crews. Even the airship was being considered for certain applications of the maritime reconnaissance and airborne early warning arts.

Perhaps the most important development in the offering in 1985 was the design study into FIMA – Future International Military Airlifter – in which British Aerospace, Lockheed, Messerschmitt and Aerospatiale were involved. The general thinking in this project was towards a C-130 (Hercules) or Starlifter shape probably, something between the two in terms of size – powered by four large fan-prop engines and capable of roles ranging from troop, vehicle and heavy-load carrying, through tanking, plus maritime reconnaissance and airborne early warning. In other words FIMA would be capable of doing everything short of fighting and bombing, perhaps even the latter occa-

Below left:
Vacu-Blast dust-free blasting equipment is used by the Major Servicing Unit at Kinloss, to remove corrosion totally before a new protective surface is applied. *Vacu-Blast*

Right:
Corrosion problems. A Nimrod mainplane main spar after 'blending out' of exfoliation corrosion.

Below:
The cross shaft main support bracket of Nimrod landing gear showing stress corrosion leading to cracks.

Below centre and bottom:
The upper surface of the rear spar of a Nimrod centre section showing exfoliation corrosion.

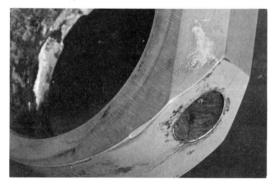

sionally. The general concept envisages the air forces of the Western world being equipped with only two basic types of combat aeroplane – those in the Tornado configuration performing all the aggressive overland tasks from fighter interception to nuclear bombing, others in the FIMA shape doing the rest.

Any forcasting about the shape and the timing of a Nimrod successor must of course depend to some extent upon predictions about the fatigue life of the existing airframes, and in such calculations the corrosion factor has to play an important part. Based on current fleet utilisation the fatigue life of all the Nimrods is judged to be satisfactory up to about 2005. Other factors which will influence 'the life of the Nimrod' include the operational adequacy of the current fit of navigation and tactical sensors by the 'Year X'; the cost of the logistic support of the aircraft, particularly of the equipments and systems which go back to Comet days; and the cost of fuel burn. The Spey engines are thirsty compared with present day and future engine/propeller/fan combinations.

The fatigue test programmes operating by 1985 fell into two parts, one set being conducted in the air from RAF Kinloss, the other on the ground in a static rig at BAe Woodford. Many previous fatigue test systems conducted by BAe and its predecessor companies had not been able fully to take into account the energetic manoeuvres performed by Service aircraft compared with the average day in the life of an airliner. In particular maritime aircraft operate in atmospheric conditions – such as low level salt laden spray – which can consume fatigue life at a relatively high rate.

A measuring system which could be installed in a Service aircraft for a period of a year or more was thought to be desirable at a fairly early stage in Nimrod's career. This would enable data to be gathered from 'true situations' particularly so far as wing stresses were concerned.

A system, designated Nimrod Operational Flight Load Measurement Programme (NOFLMP), was designed, and equipment for it installed into Nimrod XV227 at Woodford during this aeroplane's conversion from Mk 1 to Mk 2. The equipment remained in this aircraft up to the time of writing and XV227 was flying regularly from Kinloss on all normal duties, the readings from its special equipment being stored and later examined. The NOFLMP recording installation occupies part of the normal sonobuoy storage area aft of the galley. One of the problems facing Mr W.G. Heath, Chief Structural Engineer at BAe Woodford, in setting up the NOFLMP programme was determining the location of the strain guage bridges to go into XV227. It was essential that they should respond discreetly to the inputs they were designed to measure and not be influenced unduly by other inputs. Fortunately a 'retired' RAF Comet was available at Farnborough and a loading rig was used

Left:

A No 42 Squadron aircraft at Gibraltar during a NATO exercise. *RAF*

to ensure that the best positions were found. The equipment in XV227 generates a total of 45 million pieces of information per flying hour.

The second fatigue test programme involved the allocation to Woodford of 'dear old XV148', the first Nimrod prototype. After many years of test and development flying XV148 finally came back from Bedford in 1982 to have her nose and tail chopped off, making a total fuselage length of 70ft. The wing structure was carefully modified to make it fully representative of a production standard aircraft. She was then permanently installed in a made-to-measure building as the Nimrod Fatigue Test Specimen. She seems destined to stand there for many years, still with her original Comet 4 windows, with batteries of hydraulic jacks flexing her wings to the programmed orders of Mr Heath's team, the effects being minutely recorded and analysed by all that is latest and best in the world of instrumentation. The researchers can feed in almost any sort of stress that a flying Nimrod is likely to encounter, including that induced by heavy weather or even by a heavy-handed pilot. Out of it all will come decisions affecting the life-span of the whole fleet.

The whole matter of life-span could also be affected by the corrosion factor – corrosion being defined as 'the tendency of a metal to revert to a more stable natural state.'

Maritime aircraft, both fixed and rotary-winged, are obviously more susceptible than most to the ravages of corrosion since much of it has to do with the passage of electric currents, with salt water a better conductor than fresh. A sneaky form of corrosion to which maritime aircraft are especially susceptible is called 'exfoliation', often resulting from salt water condensation inside the aeroplane in the least accessible places. It is difficult to detect and the areas most affected are skin cut-out edges such as fuel tank access panels, edges of wheel wells and depressions where the saline solution

Below:

The hostile environment contributing to corrosion problems in any maritime aeroplane low level flying, with salt-laden spray rising from a rough sea. *BAe*

does not drain away and moisture becomes trapped due to lack of ventilation. In large aircraft like Nimrods, toilet and galley floors can become danger areas with the additional hazards of spillage of various liquids which can cause microbiological corrosion. The landing gear of heavy aircraft is also susceptible. When corrosion occurs in a highly stressed area of the airframe not only is there an effect on the strength of that area but consideration has to be given to the potential effect on fatigue life.

Senior engineers within both BAe and the RAF expressed confidence in 1985 that the acknowledged corrosion problems so far as Nimrod was concerned, were well under control, measures ranging from the high pressure washing of every aircraft between flights, the liberal use of water-displacing fluids such as PX-24, constant vigilance and 'good husbandry' by air and ground crews.

The reporting of potentially dangerous exposure to salt-laden spray was also an important standard operating procedure in the MR squadrons.

Taking into account all the above factors the predictable future life of Nimrod seemed at the time of writing to be a long one. Nearly 15 years after entry into RAF operational service and 35 years on from the first flights of its Comet progenitor the predicted 1990s future for Nimrod seemed a modest one.

Certainly there were very few complaints about the aeroplane from its users.

NIMROD
THE MIGHTY HUNTER

Mk 3 XZ287 at Woodford Air Show in 1982. *Dr Alan Curry*

The author looks at '227' at Kinloss on a wintry day towards the close of his research work on this volume.
Author's collection

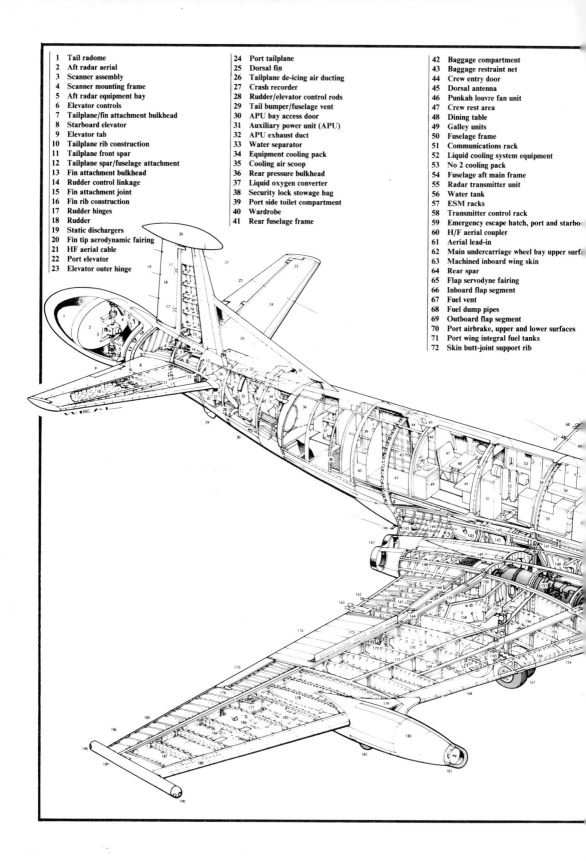

1 Tail radome
2 Aft radar aerial
3 Scanner assembly
4 Scanner mounting frame
5 Aft radar equipment bay
6 Elevator controls
7 Tailplane/fin attachment bulkhead
8 Starboard elevator
9 Elevator tab
10 Tailplane rib construction
11 Tailplane front spar
12 Tailplane spar/fuselage attachment
13 Fin attachment bulkhead
14 Rudder control linkage
15 Fin attachment joint
16 Fin rib construction
17 Rudder hinges
18 Rudder
19 Static dischargers
20 Fin tip aerodynamic fairing
21 HF aerial cable
22 Port elevator
23 Elevator outer hinge

24 Port tailplane
25 Dorsal fin
26 Tailplane de-icing air ducting
27 Crash recorder
28 Rudder/elevator control rods
29 Tail bumper/fuselage vent
30 APU bay access door
31 Auxiliary power unit (APU)
32 APU exhaust duct
33 Water separator
34 Equipment cooling pack
35 Cooling air scoop
36 Rear pressure bulkhead
37 Liquid oxygen converter
38 Security lock stowage bag
39 Port side toilet compartment
40 Wardrobe
41 Rear fuselage frame

42 Baggage compartment
43 Baggage restraint net
44 Crew entry door
45 Dorsal antenna
46 Punkah louvre fan unit
47 Crew rest area
48 Dining table
49 Galley units
50 Fuselage frame
51 Communications rack
52 Liquid cooling system equipment
53 No 2 cooling pack
54 Fuselage aft main frame
55 Radar transmitter unit
56 Water tank
57 ESM racks
58 Transmitter control rack
59 Emergency escape hatch, port and starbo
60 H/F aerial coupler
61 Aerial lead-in
62 Main undercarriage wheel bay upper surf
63 Machined inboard wing skin
64 Rear spar
65 Flap servodyne fairing
66 Inboard flap segment
67 Fuel vent
68 Fuel dump pipes
69 Outboard flap segment
70 Port airbrake, upper and lower surfaces
71 Port wing integral fuel tanks
72 Skin butt-joint support rib